Fashioning the feminine

Girls, popular culture and schooling

Pam Gilbert and
Sandra Taylor

Australian Cultural Studies
Editor: John Tulloch

ALLEN & UNWIN

First published 1991
Second impression 1992
Allen & Unwin Pty Ltd
8 Napier Street, North Sydney NSW 2059 Australia

National Library of Australia
Cataloguing-in-Publication entry:

Gilbert, Pam, 1946–
    Fashioning the feminine: girls,
    popular culture and schooling.

    Bibliography.
    Includes index.
    ISBN 0 04 442337 3.

    1. Sexism in education.   2. Sexism and
    literature.   3. Sexism in mass media.
    4. Sex role in literature.   I. Taylor,
    Sandra.   II. Title.

370.19345

Set in 10.5/11.5pt Palatino by Graphicraft Typesetters Ltd., Hong Kong

Produced by SRM Production Services Sdn Bhd, Malaysia

Fashioning the feminine

Previous titles in the series

National Fictions
Literature, film and the construction of Australian narrative
Graeme Turner

Myths of Oz
Reading Australian popular culture
John Fiske, Bob Hodge and Graeme Turner

Australian Television
Programs, pleasures and politics
John Tulloch and Graeme Turner (eds)

Contents

Acknowledgements

Many thanks to Lyn Martinez and Meridee Cuthill for their constructive criticism throughout the project; to the young women we interviewed for their time and their candour; to Michael Gilbert, Rebecca Gilbert, Rob Gilbert, Trish Mercer, and to Michelle Taylor, Julie Taylor, Colin Symes for their patience and encouragement; and to feminist friends and colleagues for their support and inspiration.

Thanks also to the School of Education at James Cook University of North Queensland for financial support.

Introduction

Much has been written in the last decade or so about the ways in which popular cultural texts construct and legitimate particular images of femininity and masculinity. Video clips, magazines, television soaps, the lyrics of popular music, dance forms, comics, formula novels, movies: the data base is rich and extensive and the analyses that result are telling and powerful indicators of the role cultural texts play in the construction of these images. At the same time, but in a rather different group of discourses, much has been written about the need for schools to provide space in classrooms for the lived experiences of students. The argument is that what counts as an acceptable classroom text must be extended; that schools must work with the popular and relevant; that educators must acknowledge the value of the wider textual experiences students bring with them to the classroom.

It is what happens when these two positions merge that is of interest to us. How readily can the dominant discourses of the classroom work with issues as complex as the role of the popular cultural text in the lives of teenage girls? What might be both the potential and the danger of such a meeting? What, for instance, is the opportunity for counter-hegemonic practice when popular cultural texts become authorised classroom texts? How well-equipped are the dominant pedagogical discourses of reading and writing to deal with such texts? And, in particular, what value might there be for young women, in terms of a meeting between popular cultural texts and the classroom, for the development of concepts of critical social literacy and cultural understanding?

We profess to some concern about the ways in which dominant classroom language discourses—steeped as they are in concepts of romanticism, individualism, and personal

1

creativity—will work with popular cultural texts. To compli-
cate this potential difficulty, we want to point to another
dimension of the meeting of cultural texts and classroom
language practices. Much has been written about the reproduction of gender inequalities through schooling practices,
about the ways in which school systems and school 'knowledge' perpetuate and construct certain images of femininity
and masculinity. The meeting of popular cultural texts and
classroom practices does not take place in a neutral arena.
How might the site for this proposed meeting influence the
way in which texts are deconstructed and reconstructed? Will
it indeed be advantageous to young women if popular cultural
forms are worked with in classrooms?

In this book we argue that popular cultural texts play a
significant role in the construction of femininity, and that such
texts work in a complex relationship with young women's
conscious—and unconscious—desires. However, we also
argue that notions of femininity are imperfectly held: they are
not static, fixed, or determined. There are always spaces for
opposition and resistance in the construction of gendered
subjectivity, and it is these spaces that can be of value for
a feminist classroom practice. Consequently, in this book we
initially consider the way in which cultural texts are 'made', in
patriarchal consumer culture, in the sub-cultures of young
women, and in the dominant culture of the classroom. We
then re-read some of the popular cultural texts, in terms of
other 'readings' that might be more advantageous to young
women. Television soaps, romance series novels, and the
copious (and seldom considered) texts that young women
write at school are considered in terms of their relationships
to the discourses that produced them, and in terms of their
potential for counter-hegemonic practice. The argument is
finally made for the need for feminist pedagogical practices
which can work constructively—and deconstructively—with
cultural texts in the classroom. The final section of the book
looks at what should inform such practice, and at what re-
sources might help in such a task.

Part I

Making the texts

1

The cultural construction of femininity: gender relations, schooling and popular culture

...no one asked me to dance. I sat there smiling, the smile going stiff...I'd made a world of my own, a retreat, but at the dance it couldn't save me. It was my body decked out in raspberry nylon and once I'd liked everything about it...But now, after the dance, it was something to be ashamed of. It didn't seem that it was my body—I couldn't get free of my failure and feel cosy inside it. The shame had got inside me. Only boys counted and they didn't want me and I was afraid. (Hanrahan, 1984, quoted in Gilbert, 1988b: p. 74)

In this first section of the book we will outline a framework for exploring the roles played by popular culture and schooling in the construction of femininity, and consider why the cultural construction of femininity is an important and relevant issue for the classroom. The basic starting point of our work is that while schooling is a site for the reproduction of gender relations, it is also a site for intervention and change. Our concern is to understand the processes involved in the construction of femininity in order to develop classroom practices by which they might be challenged. We are centrally interested in the role played by cultural texts in the construction of femininity, and in the ways in which such texts relate to the lived experiences of teenage girls. Before turning to a specific focus on textuality and classroom practice in chapter 2, this chapter will consider the broader context of gender relations of which schooling is a part, and clarify relevant theoretical issues, in particular the approach to be taken to cultural studies.

Cultural processes are integrally related to the social structure and to power relations, and are important in reproducing the gender-based inequalities which characterise the social structure in Australia and New Zealand, as well as in the UK and USA. For example, although school retention rates in contemporary Australia have improved for girls since 1975, when girls were first identified as a 'disadvantaged group' educationally, girls still leave school with limited options compared with boys as a result of their school experiences. Subjects studied still show traditional sex differences, and girls are still less likely than boys to study mathematics and science (NSW Ministry of Education and Youth Affairs, 1988). They are also less likely to obtain post-school qualifications of any kind. Apprenticeship and trade courses, which are more likely to be entered by working-class students, are still almost totally the preserve of males: only 12.2 per cent of all apprentices in Australia are female (NSW Ministry of Education and Youth Affairs, 1988). Further, in terms of tertiary participation, sex-differentiated patterns still exist, with female school leavers more likely to enter humanities oriented and teacher education courses at colleges of advanced education, and less likely than males to enrol in either high status courses or higher degree courses at university level (DEET, 1989). One of the consequences of this is that Australia has one of the most gender segmented labour markets among comparable countries. In addition, women's full-time average earnings are still only 79 per cent of those of men (Women's Bureau, 1989), and the economic recession and labour market changes of recent years have made young women particularly vulnerable. In many ways these women have fewer options than in the past and have become increasingly vulnerable to welfare dependency and poverty (Taylor, 1986).

We are interested in how the cultural sphere relates to these social inequalities. In particular, we wish to explore how cultural texts are involved in reproducing gender ideologies and in what ways they might be used in the classroom to challenge these ideologies. Although we acknowledge that broad policies are needed to address structural inequalities in Australia, we would argue that school-based and culturally focussed approaches are also important.

Theorising culture

The approach we take to cultural studies is interdisciplinary—drawing particularly on sociology, feminist theory, literary theory and media studies. Because cultural studies is such a wide field, some clarification of the terms to be used is needed. In particular it is necessary to offer a conceptualisation of culture—'that most important and slippery concept of all' (Fiske, 1987: p. 20). We draw on John Fiske's work in explaining an approach to culture:

> Culture is concerned with meanings and pleasures: our culture consists of the meanings we make of our social experience and of our social relations, and therefore the sense we have of our 'selves'. It also situates those meanings within the social system, for a social system can only be held in place by the meanings that people make of it. Culture is deeply inscribed in the differential distribution of power within a society, for power relations can only be stabilized or destabilized by the meanings that people make of them. Culture is a struggle for meanings as society is a struggle for power. (1987: p. 20)

This definition captures nicely the relationship between culture and social structure, and between meanings and power relations, for meanings and their circulation are 'part and parcel of [the] social structure' (Fiske, 1987: p. 1). It also emphasises the dynamic nature of cultural processes where people as agents are involved in shaping the social structure, as well as the notion of 'the sense we have of ourselves', which is of central importance. We will discuss this in more depth later in this chapter.

This, then, is part of the framework for our work: we are interested in the generation and circulation of meanings, in this case meanings relating to gender, and how these meanings are implicated in the construction of femininity in girls and young women. Such meanings are organised at a number of interrelated levels within a dynamic ideological system. In relation to the construction of femininity we will refer to *discourse* about gender as 'a language or system of representation that has developed socially in order to make and circulate a coherent set of meanings about an important topic area' (Fiske, 1987: p. 14). At a broader level such coherent sets of meanings may be referred to as *ideologies*, although both discourses and ideologies operate in a dynamic ideological field: ideologies 'do not operate through single ideas; they operate in discursive chains, in clusters, in semantic fields, in discursive formations' (Hall, 1985).

Within this framework, cultural texts are part of a network of meanings which constitute the social world and which may be viewed as sites of struggle over meaning. Following Leslie Roman and Linda Christian-Smith (1988), our definition of *cultural text* includes both representational forms (for example a video clip or a teen magazine) and lived social relations (for example of a specific group such as Greek girls in a high school). Although these two types of cultural text are separable analytically, they are closely interrelated in everyday social practice.

Another 'slippery' term which we need to define is *popular culture*. Various definitions with differing emphases have developed historically and as Roman and Christian-Smith observe:

> Popular culture is a concept prone to...slippages and is so easily saleable that it serves the purpose of those who wish to defend it as the authentic experiences of everyday people and those who see it as representing the ways in which the masses are duped into their own manipulation by the so-called cultural industries, or even those who simply celebrate its relation to the sensory, the immediate, or the visceral impulses of contemporary social life (1988: p. 9).

In the context of our focus on meaning and the construction of femininity, Stuart Hall's (1981) view of popular culture as a site of struggle where 'the people' are constituted is useful. (See also Johnson, 1986.) Central in Hall's approach is the tension between the forces of domination which attempt to define 'the people' and the resistances to these imposed definitions. Drawing on Hall's work, and also on unpublished work by John Clarke, Roman and Christian-Smith (1988) argue that there is a need for an alternative position to both the 'cultural populism' and 'pessimism' approaches to popular culture which are reflected in the above quotation: an alternative position which recognises that structural conditions set limits on consumer resistance to popular cultural forms. Such conditions may prevent any opposition from becoming politically effective, constraining it to passive forms of dissent.

Gender and culture

The general approach to culture and meaning, culture and power relations, and to popular culture outlined above can be related to a specific consideration of gender issues.

Gender relations

An understanding of the reproduction of gender relations needs to take account of the links between personal lives and social structures, in other words to consider how everyday social practices constitute social structure. R.W. Connell's (1986; 1987) practice-based theory is useful here in that it takes account of structural dimensions and also historical change in gender relations. Following Jill Matthews (1984), Connell uses the concept 'gender order' which he defines as 'a historically constructed pattern of power relations between men and women' (1987: p. 99). Feminist theorising has often used the concept of patriarchy to refer to a single overarching structure of domination (see Eisenstein, 1984; Burton, 1985), but Connell argues that this over-simplifies the structures of gender relations and he offers instead three major structures focussed around the division of labour, the power relations between men and women, and sexuality. While Connell sees these structures as separable analytically, he claims they are closely interwoven in a dynamic way in social life. We accept this view of the complexity of the gender order, but would argue that the concept of patriarchy—a concept central to the theorising of women's oppression—needs to be retained. Hence we use the term *patriarchal gender order*.

Within this broad framework of the gender order we can view various institutional settings, such as schools, families and the workplace, where social practices are gender structured. Connell refers to the state of play in such settings as the 'gender regime' (1987: p. 120). Cultural texts of all kinds are a part of the gender regime in various institutional settings. For example in a school setting, as well as in the family or in the street, there will be a network of interrelating cultural texts, both representational and 'lived'.

Also associated with everyday gendered practices are appropriate definitions of femininity and masculinity which help to maintain, and in turn are shaped by, the patriarchal gender order. These understandings of what it means to be female or male, which are implicated in all aspects of social life, develop in relation to each other in particular historical and social situations. Gender 'only has meaning when the concepts of masculinity and femininity are recognized as a pair which exist in a relationship of complementarity and antithesis' (MacDonald, 1981: p. 160).

These understandings of what it means to be female or male do not rest on biological differences. As Connell convincingly argues: 'There must be...a really thorough rejection of the notion that natural difference *is* a basis of gender, that the social patterns are somehow an *elaboration* of natural difference ...Social gender relations do not *express* natural patterns; they *negate* the biological statute' (1986: pp. 354–5). He points out that gender differences, rather than expressing natural differences, actually suppress natural *similarities*. And gender ideologies such as femininity and masculinity help to 'naturalise' gender differences so that they are seen as 'given' and inevitable. Societies where the gender order is patriarchal, such as contemporary western societies, are characterised by what Connell describes as 'emphasised femininity' and 'hegemonic masculinity' (1987: p. 183). Hegemonic masculinity is constructed in relation to the dominance of men over women, as well as over other forms of masculinity. It is heterosexual and tends to be characterised by power, authority, aggression and technical competence (p. 187). On the other hand, emphasised femininity, the form of femininity which complements hegemonic masculinity, is characterised by compliance with subordination and is oriented to accommodating the interests and desires of men. Associated with emphasised femininity are qualities of sociability, sexual passivity and acceptance of domesticity and motherhood (p. 187).

A number of versions of femininity and masculinity are constructed in everyday social practices within institutions, but at a broad cultural level the versions promoted provide the basis for women's subordination. Thus we see emphasised femininity and hegemonic masculinity represented at the symbolic level in the mass media as the cultural ideals. Connell comments on the relationship between everyday gendered practices and the historically constructed cultural ideals: 'The ideological representations of femininity draw on, but do not necessarily correspond to, actual femininities as they are lived. What most women support is not necessarily what they are' (p. 186). Connell asserts that the forms of femininity and masculinity constructed at the ideological level tend to be 'stylized and impoverished', but that 'their interrelation is centred on a single structural fact, the global dominance of men over women' (p. 183).

In theorising gender relations it is necessary also to take account of other major power relations such as class and ethnicity, and of the ways in which the patriarchal gender order is integrated with capitalism. There have been numerous theoretical debates in the literature about the relationship between capitalism and patriarchy, and between marxism and feminism, which have been further complicated by the different positions taken by radical, liberal, and socialist feminists (Eisenstein, 1984). To some extent these issues remain unsolved. In a general sense, our view is that patriarchy and capitalism have developed together historically to take on particular structural forms in contemporary Australia, and that these structures have also been shaped by colonialism and immigration. Zillah Eisenstein (1979) refers to the particular structural form which has developed in societies like Australia as a 'capitalist patriarchy'.

Madeleine MacDonald has provided a useful analysis from a marxist feminist perspective of the way in which capitalism and patriarchy are integrated. She suggests that:

> . . . both class relations and gender relations, while they exist within their own histories, can nevertheless be so closely interwoven that it is theoretically very difficult to draw them apart within specific historic conjunctures. The development of capitalism is one such conjuncture where one finds patriarchal relations of dominance and control over women buttressing the structure of class domination. (1981: p. 160)

In her view, class domination under capitalism is supported by male dominance over women in the workplace, in the family and in public life. At the same time, class relations limit and structure gender relations and associated gender identities. The dominance of men in the workplace is sustained by the reproductive role of women as child bearers and rearers in the patriarchal family, and the ideological split between the 'public sphere' of men and the 'private sphere' of women helps to maintain the view that childcare and domestic labour are women's work. MacDonald argues that the public/private split is also a major factor in the reproduction of the sex-segregated workforce characteristic of the capitalist mode of production. She claims that: 'What it is important to recognise is that the congruence of these two structures is not natural but socially imposed and, as a result, has to be continually reinforced through the legal, political and educational agencies of the state, if it is to be maintained' (1981: p.161). The ways in which this occurs through schooling will be discussed later in this chapter.

While class and gender relations operate dynamically at a structural level they are also interrelated in social practices and institutions and, with ethnicity, shape women's experiences differentially. It is important, therefore, that women's experience is not universalised and that women and girls are not referred to as homogenous groups. There are, for example, differences in the experiences and degree of subordination of white middle-class Anglo-Australian women and Aboriginal women. Aboriginal women are likely to be triply oppressed on the basis of class, race and gender, though for many their major struggle is still against racist oppression and its effects, both at a personal and institutional level (Neill, 1989).

Popular culture and femininity

Gender ideologies are crucial in sustaining the patriarchal gender order and cultural texts play an important role in promoting the dominant forms of femininity and masculinity at a symbolic level. We are particularly interested in the images of femininity represented in the popular cultural texts that are part of the everyday world of teenage girls. Such texts, as we have explained, can be viewed as *representational cultural texts* and play an important part in the struggle over meanings in the popular cultural field.

Rosemary Pringle's (1983) attempt to theorise the links between sexuality and consumption in post-war Australia is particularly relevant to a discussion of the role of popular culture in the construction of femininity, (see also Game and Pringle, 1979). Pringle traces the increasing sexualisation of women's bodies in the media from the 1920s, a trend which became more direct and all encompassing in the post-war period. Accompanying the movement of women from the paid workforce back to the home, advertisers began to associate products with love and romance, and women were increasingly encouraged to consume to become attractive to men. Pringle suggests that sexuality was restructured in relation to consumption in ways which '...assumed emotional, and later sexual, connotations as the arena of personal fulfilment and individual meaning' (1983: p. 90). As a consequence of this restructuring, consumption has come to be seen as a way of completing the ideal feminine identity. For older women that identity centres on the domestic sphere and on being the perfect wife and mother. For young women, however, the focus is on appearance and looks and on being the perfect sex object. Both of these ideals require that women become consumers; that they acquire particular products that will make them desirable—either as wife or sex object. The message of advertising being that 'to be able to buy is the same thing as being sexually desirable' (Berger, 1972: p. 144). As Pringle argues, certain products, such as cosmetics, are thus seen as being essential to femininity. This is in contrast with male products, which are seen as compatible with, but never essential to, masculinity.

A further important aspect of the construction of sexuality under consumer capitalism is that femininity has come to be associated with passive sexuality, with being touched and being looked at; masculinity, on the other hand, is defined more actively, and involves touching and looking (Game and Pringle, 1979: p. 11). In a much-quoted passage John Berger refers to the way in which these aspects are reflected in the social construction of femininity:

> A woman must continually watch herself. She is almost continually accompanied by her own image of herself...From earliest childhood she has been taught and persuaded to survey herself continually.
> And so she comes to consider the surveyor and the surveyed within her as the two constituent yet always distinct elements of her identity as a woman.
> She has to survey everything she is and everything she does because how she appears to others, and ultimately how she appears to men, is of crucial importance for what is normally thought of as the success of her life. (1972: p. 46)

Berger goes on to make the important point that the surveyor of woman in herself is male. 'Thus she turns herself into an object—and most particularly an object of vision: a sight' (p. 47).

This focus on appearance and sexuality has particular relevance for the construction of femininity in young women and girls and helps to explain why the body tends to be taken on as a project. Rosalind Coward contends that the camera in contemporary media has been put to use as an extension of the male gaze on women, with the result that the development of female identity is fraught with anxiety and enmeshed with judgements about desirability. Thus the emphasis on women's looks 'becomes a crucial way in which society exercises control over women's sexuality' (1984: p. 77). To 'be fashionable' necessitates the achievement of current sexual ideals, and these ideals connote powerlessness and, for adolescent girls, a responsive sexuality.

The emphasis on women's looks is most apparent in women's magazines, in advertising and on television, where visual representations of women are central. However, even in cultural texts which do not rely on visual images, the import- ance of good looks and sexual attractiveness for women is likely to be a dominant textual image. In relation to girls and young women the overall message in cultural texts is that sexuality confers power—though in relation to the social and economic context this power, derived from appearance and attractiveness, is extremely limited. We will take up this last point in the next section.

Despite this overall emphasis on appearance and sexuality, it needs to be emphasised that the role which such texts play in the construction of femininity is complex. Even though the ideal of sexual submissiveness characterises 'emphasised femininity' which we discussed earlier, there is no simple transmission of a single coherent 'patriarchal ideology'. Although dominant ideologies may be pervasive, media texts reflect a range of contradictory and conflicting ideologies. In addition, we need to be cautious about too readily assuming 'effects' from readings of texts. Representational cultural texts need to be considered in the context of *lived social texts*: every- day sub-cultural social relations.

Girls' sub-cultures

To understand the framework within which teenage girls make sense of themselves, it is necessary to take account of their cultural perspectives. A number of studies of teenage girls' sub-cultures, particularly those of working-class girls, provide useful insights about the contradictions teenage girls experience and the concerns they express. This research is important not only for understanding the construction of femininity, but also for considering appropriate ways for feminist educators to work with teenage girls. Research on 'cultures of femininity' shows that teenage girls experience a number of conflicts resulting from the contradictory messages they receive about how they should behave, and it is possible to group these conflicts into three sets of contradictory discourses. While these sets of discourses are interrelated, they will be discussed separately.

The first set of contradictory discourses centres on girls' futures and can be described as the domesticity/paid work conflict. Girls face conflicting ideas about what is appropriate both in relation to their domestic futures, and to their futures in paid employment. Most recent Australian research shows that girls not only accept that they are likely to spend a significant part of their lives in paid work, but that they also know that they are likely to be involved in domesticity and child rearing (Thomas, 1980; Moran, 1983; Samuel, 1983; Wilson and Wyn, 1987).

Lois Bryson (1984) has argued that the inevitable conflict that occurs when a woman must fill roles both within the family and within the economic system creates a tension and a double bind for women, which is central in the reproduction of gender relations. It is significant that this tension looms early in teenage girls' lives. Teenage girls are more likely to be involved in domestic chores and childcare than are boys of this age, and this is particularly so in the case of working-class girls and in some migrant families (Strintzos, 1984). Christine Griffin's (1984) study of 'typical girls' in England highlighted the importance of domestic responsibilities in the lives of the girls she studied and, in fact, she suggests that they learn about their present and future positions in family life and in the labour market through these experiences. The girls experienced strong pressures to get a boyfriend and to get married; they saw marriage and motherhood as distant but inevitable events, and both working-class girls and their more 'academic' peers saw their future employment being shaped by childcare and domestic responsibilities. Most of the Australian research supports these findings and shows that, although livelihood issues are now as important to girls as to boys, it is domestic concerns which still dominate girls' thinking (for example, Thomas, 1980; Moran, 1983; Dwyer et al., 1984; Wilson and Wyn, 1987).

The second set of discourses, which we describe as the 'slags or drags' conflict, following Cowie and Lees (1981) and Lees (1986), relates to sexuality. In their study of working-class girls in Britain, Celia Cowie and Sue Lees found that the use of the label 'slag' to describe girls who were supposedly sexually available was extremely complex, with constant sliding within its usage 'as friendly joking; as bitchy abuse; as a threat or as a label' (1981: p. 18). The presence of the label acted as a powerful force in the construction of sexuality because for 'nice girls', sexual relationships were only seen to be permissible with love and romance. Cowie and Lees argue that the construction of female sexuality hinges on the difference between 'slags' and 'drags'; based on notions of overt sexuality and conventional 'decency'. Ways of behaving and dressing which were seen as sexual were deemed to be bad, and Cowie and Lees comment on 'the narrow tightrope [teenage girls] walk to achieve attractiveness without the taint of sexuality' (1981: p. 20).

These labelling practices have been termed 'the politics of reputation' (Bottomly, 1979) and have also been described in Australian studies of working-class teenage girls (for example, Samuel, 1983). Such practices are also particularly evident in some migrant girls' cultures, and research by Maria Strintzos on Greek girls in Melbourne shows the ways in which the Greek notion of 'honour' organises girls' lives in fundamental ways. For these teenage girls the tightrope to be walked was even more precarious because, while '[a] future without marriage was inconceivable', sexual involvements were absolutely taboo. 'To be Greek is to be "good"', was the code of honour which operated powerfully in the girls Strintzos studied—to be 'bad' therefore was a denial of ethnicity, as well as of an acceptable form of femininity (Strintzos, 1984: p. 30).

The third set of contradictory discourses relates to age or maturity and can be related to an adolescence/femininity conflict, as discussed by Barbara Hudson (1984). The notion of adolescence as a time of rebellion and independence has male connotations which conflict with expectations associated with femininity. While rebelliousness in teenage boys is more often tolerated, teenage girls are expected to be mature. From first menstruation girls are continually told, 'You're a young woman now', and this inevitably causes conflicts for girls in their early teens. Hudson argues that the conflicting expectations which impinge on teenage girls make it difficult for them to know what is expected of them. The effect, she reports, is that they say, 'Whatever we do, it's always wrong' (1984: p. 31).

These three related sources of conflict work together to define and construct femininity in particular ways and they do so within the private, domestic sphere. Both the slag/drag conflict and the adolescence/femininity conflict work to regulate sexuality in traditional ways—towards marriage and motherhood. They are consistent with the 'to have and to hold' discourse, associated with monogamous relationships, a discourse which is so pervasive in the construction of female subjectivity (see Hollway, 1984). For teenage girls, relationships are still usually seen in terms of marriage and motherhood; sexual behaviour is seen as only being appropriate within a context of love and/or marriage. These sexual codes create pressures on teenagers to get and keep a steady boyfriend (McRobbie, 1978; Cowie and Lees, 1981; Lees, 1986) and, because of these pressures, 'romance' emerges as a central theme in studies of the lives of teenage girls.

Unfortunately, these powerful pressures are experienced at a critical time: a time when girls could be thinking and planning for the future. Consequently, girls and young women often experience a conflict between their preoccupation with issues relating to femininity, and their awareness of educational concerns. As a result, girls often have 'romanticised' rather than 'realistic' views about their futures, and the research in this area is interesting and highly significant. Many of the teenage girls discussed in research studies *are* realistically aware of their futures, though there seem to be some interesting class differences. For example, Claire Thomas found that 'while middle-class girls sought a life partnership based on romantic love, working-class girls looked more for someone who would provide support for them and their children' (1980: p. 152). There are also ethnic differences in relation to these issues. For example, Griffin found that the Asian and Caribbean girls in her British study were more critical of the myth of romantic love than were the white girls. Significantly, in relation to their futures, the pressures to 'get a man' influenced job expectations. The girls drew a distinction between jobs like office work, which were seen as being suitably 'feminine', and factory work, which was regarded as 'not a good job for a girl'. This study shows the young women to be trapped between the demands of the sexual, marriage and labour markets (Griffin, 1984).

A Canadian study (Baker, 1985) suggests that while teenage girls may be *intellectually* aware of the fact that families break up and that there are people in poverty, they tend to feel that they themselves are immune to these forces. In spite of an awareness that they would in the future be engaged in paid work *and* raising a family, they did not seem to realise the difficulties they might have in moving in and out of the

workforce for childbearing/rearing. In terms of personal relationships, most girls portrayed marriage in romantic terms
—their marriages would last, with husbands who would be
loving and kind. Thus there was a contradiction between
their intellectual awareness about trends in society and their
personal dreams for themselves.

As well as this growing body of research concerned with
girls' sub-cultures there has also been an interest in exploring
the ways in which popular cultural texts relate to girls' lives
(McRobbie, 1978; McRobbie, 1984; Frith, 1985; Willinsky and
Hunniford, 1986). This work has usefully highlighted what is a
central issue for this book: the nature of the interrelationship
between the images of femininity in representational cultural
texts, and the lived social relations of adolescent girls. For
example, popular cultural texts such as teenage magazines are
viewed as active in the production and circulation of new
meanings for young women. As MacDonald comments: 'The
problem, therefore, is not one of trying to fit these representations of women to the realities of their lives but rather to
recognise the ideological 'work' carried out by these texts in
the *reconstruction* rather than the reproduction of gender
definitions and relations' (1981: p. 173).

Many studies show 'romance' to be a central theme in the
popular cultural texts which are part of girls' everyday lives.
For example, as we will describe in chapter 4, teen romance
novels are the most popular genre of literature read by teenage
girls in the USA, Canada and the UK, as well as in Australia.
Similarly romance is a central theme in other popular cultural
texts like magazines, soap operas and contemporary music.
Clearly 'romance' plays a major and complex role in the
processes involved in the construction of femininity, and
it is a central theme in both representational cultural texts
and girls' sub-cultures. Through romance, girls can rehearse
the contradictory messages and anxieties they experience in
their real lives, in their fantasy worlds, and in the blurred
margins between them. We explore these issues further in
chapter 4.

The economic context and the power relations with which
the cultural perspectives of teenage girls are linked need also
to be considered. Within a context of contradictory discourses,
romance seems to offer a partial solution to girls and young
women who, in many ways, have limited options. As Myra
Connell and others have argued: 'Romance represents...a
rational expression of, and response to, material and economic

subordination' (1981: p. 165). As in the past, when marriage was an escape or liberation from family life or domestic service (Alford, 1984), young working-class women today still lack economic alternatives. Thus a preoccupation with romance reflects the limited options available in the economic sphere. The appeal of romantic ideology may lie partly in the sphere of the unconscious, but it works together with material factors to lead to marriage and motherhood and, ultimately, to dependency.

Schooling and the reproduction of gender relations

In our earlier discussion on gender relations we emphasised that schools are important institutional settings for their reproduction and in particular for maintaining ideas about 'women's place' under capitalism. Gender ideologies trans-mitted through schooling are important in maintaining women's subordinate position in domestic work and in the labour market.

Detailed discussion of various theoretical approaches to the role of schooling in the reproduction of social inequalities is not appropriate here. However, two points are important in relation to theorising the reproduction of *gender relations* through schooling. Early approaches to such theorising (e.g., Bowles and Gintis, 1976; Bourdieu and Passeron, 1977) were criticised in the literature for being simplistic and deterministic and for failing to take account of resistance, negotiation and contestation (see, for example, Apple, 1982). Consequently, more recent approaches have focussed on 'the ways in which both individuals and classes assert their own experience and contest or resist the ideological and material forces imposed on them in a variety of settings' (Weiler, 1988: p. 11). Kathleen Weiler refers to analyses such as these which stress agency and resistance (e.g., Willis, 1977) as 'theories of production' in contrast to reproduction theories.

The earlier work on reproduction theory was also criticised for its failure to take account of the ways in which schooling reproduces *gender* as well as class inequalities. For example, Sam Bowles and Herb Gintis (1976) saw the sexual division of labour as originating predominantly in the home and family. The role of the domestic work of women under capitalism was acknowledged, but the reproduction of the gender divisions in the labour market was not analysed. Similarly, although Pierre

Bourdieu's *Outline of a Theory of Practice* (1977), has since been used to develop a feminist theory of production (MacDonald, 1981), his work initially focussed on the cultural reproduction of *class* relations.

MacDonald's theory is particularly relevant for our purposes here as she takes into account agency in the construction of both class and gender identities in schools. She also highlights the need to focus on 'the cultural framework within which individuals find a sense of themselves' (MacDonald, 1981: p. 163). A number of studies have taken this approach and have attempted to explore issues relating to gender and education in their wider cultural context. Such feminist work has often explored the lived experiences of girls within and outside school, so highlighting the diversity and complexity of experiences of girls and women in schools. For example, Angela McRobbie (1978) and Claire Thomas (1980) have explored the complexities of class and gender, while Mary Fuller (1980) and Alison Jones (1988) have documented ethnic differences in girls' school experiences. In general such studies have been concerned with 'the ways in which girls, both individually and collectively, make sense of and try to negotiate oppressive social relationships and structures in order to gain more control over their own lives' (Weiler, 1988: pp. 45–6). These studies have utilised concepts of resistance and accommodation in attempting to understand how girls and women actively respond to oppression rather than passively internalise dominant ideologies, and recent work clearly demonstrates both the awareness girls have of their social situation and their ability to make rational choices about their lives (Wilson and Wyn, 1987). Our work has been influenced by approaches such as these, which put the perspectives and concerns of girls and young women themselves at the centre of attention.

Femininity and school processes

Notions of femininity and masculinity have long been recognised as central in schooling, even though they have been promoted more subtly in recent times. Historically, however, the education of girls and boys has been overtly and explicitly different, as it has been based on supposed 'natural' differences and differences in life roles. In general, the formal education of girls was seen to be less important than the education of boys and was therefore limited and narrowly defined. As each stage of formal educational provision developed (primary/secondary/tertiary), it was first made available for boys and later extended to girls. Students were placed in different schools, or rigidly separated where the same building was used, and this division was reflected in the different curricula which were taught (Kyle, 1986).

There were also class differences in the educational opportunities available to girls which affected participation rates, and although many boys and girls were engaged in paid work, working-class daughters often remained at home to help with domestic work (Kyle, 1986). In addition, middle-class girls were more likely to move to secondary schooling, often in catholic and private schools. But despite class differences in education, strong ideological pressures ensured that in general all women were prepared for future domestic roles as dependents of men. This ignored the fact that many women, particularly working-class women, were engaged in paid work. For example, a survey of women in employment in Melbourne in the 1880s showed the extent of women's involvement in domestic service and economic activity. As well as 47 per cent who were in domestic service of some description, 37 per cent were in manufacturing (particularly in the clothing industry), and the rest in commercial and professional categories (Grimshaw, 1986: pp. 199–200). However, powerful gender ideologies held that women's 'proper place' was within the domestic sphere and that only men were breadwinners. As a result, women's wages were set at lower rates than those of men, and the existence of the many women who were in fact supporting their families was ignored.

For many years, the schooling of girls reflected these ideas about 'women's place'. Middle-class girls were taught 'the accomplishments'—for example, music, singing and drawing—while working-class girls were trained for domestic labour, either as servants or as future wives and mothers. However, both working-class and middle-class girls were taught sewing and domestic science at the expense of other subjects. Domestic science was viewed as a way to ensure that 'as many working-class girls as possible were inculcated with the precepts of industry, thrift, self sacrifice and morality' (Kyle, 1986: p. 53). Academic subjects were only taught in elite private schools, and in convent schools, but the emphasis on domestic science was actively resisted by parents and students in state schools who demanded courses, such as commercial courses, which would prepare their girls for the new vocational areas opening up at the beginning of the twentieth century (Kyle, 1986; Porter, 1983). This ideology of 'women's place' has persisted in various ways and is still reflected in contemporary secondary schooling. For example, home economics is still seen as a 'feminine' subject primarily associated with women's domestic lives, while physics and chemistry are seen as 'masculine'.

The construction of femininity and masculinity in secondary schools continues processes which begin in the family, and are reinforced by the primary school experiences of children (Delamont, 1980; Evans, 1982, 1988). In both primary and secondary schooling, teachers' expectations about different interests, abilities and likely futures of girls and boys are subtly conveyed through classroom practice and some of these processes will be described more fully in chapter 2, where we focus on the role of language practices in the construction of femininity. It is through the 'hidden curriculum' that many unintended and unexamined messages are passed through school processes, and this level is at least as powerful in its effects as the official curriculum. For example, Nancy Lesko (1988) has documented the ways in which the 'total ensemble of school experiences and messages' become in effect a 'curriculum of the body' which is implicated in social control and the legitimation of certain versions of femininity.

At the secondary level the official curriculum uses gender as a segregating factor in a most obvious way in single-sex schools and in single-sex classes, but there are many other ways in which curriculum and school organisation promote dominant gender ideologies. Here subject offerings and timetabling are important, as schools may force traditional choices by, for example, timetabling subjects such as manual arts and home economics at the same time slot. Dominant gender ideologies are also transmitted through various resource materials and through classroom interaction, as we will describe more fully in chapter 2. MacDonald has argued that 'the message of school texts is most likely to represent in its purest form the ideological statement of the ruling class or, at least, those values which it considers essential to transmit.' (1981: p. 172). In reviewing research on the representation of women in school texts, MacDonald highlights three main themes which emerge: women's invisibility and passivity, the under-representation of women in paid work and their concentration in low-status occupations, and an insistent emphasis on female domesticity. In relation to this last point, MacDonald comments that: 'The message comes across not as any subtle or hidden code but rather with a degree of repetition that can only be described as ideological bombardment' (p. 171).

The dynamics of classroom interaction has also consistently shown that in the primary school, teachers demonstrate a preference for boys, interact more with them and value male ideas more highly (Delamont, 1980; Evans, 1982; Spender, 1982), while at the secondary school level, both male and female teachers give boys more attention and are apparently unaware that they are doing so (Schools Commission, 1984; Stanworth, 1984; Kelly, 1985). It may well be through classroom interaction that girls receive the most powerful messages about 'women's place'.

However, we have stressed that gender ideologies are not passively internalised but are actively negotiated and resisted by girls and women, and a number of feminist research studies have documented how working-class girls in particular resist the official gender ideology of the school. For example, McRobbie's (1978) study of working-class girls showed how they developed an anti-school sub-culture which was also antagonistic to middle-class girls. These girls asserted their femaleness in the classroom by introducing sexuality in such a way as to force teachers to take notice. McRobbie describes how the official school image of femininity (neatness and passivity) was rejected in favour of a more feminine, even sexual one, with the girls wearing makeup to school and disrupting the class by loud discussions about boyfriends.

In an Australian study of two girls' state schools in Melbourne, one working-class and one middle-class, Thomas (1980) found some interesting differences. Both groups of girls turned towards traditional female roles in their efforts to resist the academic demands of the school and to achieve positive identities which challenged the negative ones placed on them by the school. However, Thomas found middle-class girls much more subdued in their opposition to school than the working-class girls, who saw school as a hostile and repressive institution. Working-class girls constructed an image of themselves as 'tough, worldly and unromantic' and were much more 'anti-school' in their attitudes and behaviour. Linley Samuel (1983) also found, in her study of working-class girls in Sydney, that traditional notions of femininity were rejected by the girls, who instead used their sexuality as an effective weapon in the classroom. However, the teachers responded by labelling the girls as 'promiscuous', writing them off, and encouraging them to drop out of school. Samuel also reports that despite such strong rebelliousness, these girls could not see any real futures for themselves outside marriage.

It is likely that, as with working-class boys, opposition to school leads working-class girls to a traditional working-class future. Willis's (1977) 'lads', in opposing school values, qualified themselves for futures as manual workers. However, for them manual work confirmed their masculinity and thereby gave them status. But in the case of girls, status is not achieved from 'women's work', and in the long run girls see few alternatives to motherhood and childrearing, whether they be with or without love, romance and marriage.

Construction of feminine subjectivity

We have emphasised that gender ideologies are central in the reproduction of gender relations, and we have also suggested that we need a theoretical approach which takes account of the relationship between everyday practices and social structures. One crucial issue which we have not discussed so far is the formation of gender identity at the personal level. We need to understand how it is that gender ideologies continue to *work* at a personal level, and why women apparently consent to their own subordination.

Recent theorists interested in the relationship between the individual and social structure have tended to replace the notion of 'the individual' with that of 'the subject' (Beechy and Donald, 1985; Henriques et al., 1984). The distinction between these two concepts is relevant to the notion of 'sense of self'. While 'the individual' is viewed as being essentially biological, the notion of 'the subject' highlights the 'constructed sense of the individual in a network of social relations' (Fiske, 1987: p. 48). Thus, from this perspective, a sense of identity which is socially constructed is referred to as *subjectivity*, in contrast to *individuality*, which is the product of nature or biology:

> Our subjectivity, then, is the product of social relations that work upon us in three main ways, through society, through language or discourse, and through psychic processes through which the infant enters into society, language and consciousness. Our subjectivity is...the product of the various social agencies to which we are subject, and thus is what we share with others. (Fiske, 1987: p. 49)

This approach to subjectivity is particularly useful in exploring constructions of femininity, because it explains the contradictory ways in which gender ideologies are experienced at various levels. For example, we have already commented on the fact that for teenage girls there may be a contradiction between their intellectual awareness about trends in society, and their personal dreams for themselves. Similarly, there may be a contradiction about having children: 'It is neither a question of free choice, nor of false consciousness. For example, women can recognise child-rearing as restricting and oppressive and yet still want to bear children' (Henriques et al., 1984: p. 220). However, while it is important to acknowledge the way in which gender ideologies work at an unconscious level through the structuring of desires, it is also important to understand that these desires are produced and are therefore potentially changeable. Some of the ways in which these desires are produced will be considered in the discussions of specific cultural texts in Part II of this book. In chapter 6 we then consider the development of a feminist classroom practice through which some of the processes involved in the reproduction of patriarchal gender relations might be challenged.

2

The pedagogical construction of femininity: textuality and the classroom

> They will not forgive us
> These girls
> Sitting in serried rows
> Hungry for attention
> Like shelves of unread books,
> If we do not
> Make the world new for them,
> Teach them to walk
> Into the possibilities
> Of their own becoming,
> Confident in their exploring.
> (from *Classroom Politics* by Fiona Norris, 1985)

In an attempt to tease out both the well known and the lesser known aspects of the school's role in the perpetuation of gendered subjectivity, this second chapter focusses on the way in which particular classroom *language* practices perpetuate patriarchal ideologies in seemingly invisible and innocent ways. This is an important focus to take, given that the school's dealings with popular cultural texts (texts like those which will be described later in this book), take place mostly in the language classroom. Many popular texts are indeed authorised and adopted for school work and bought by school libraries and media units. In other words, they are 'read' in schools, and written about in schools.

Schools are involved in the transmission of many cultural texts, but as the collection of papers edited by Suzanne de Castell, Allan Luke and Carmen Luke (1989) demonstrates, the complexities and subtleties of transmission cannot be underestimated. It is not only the apparent content of textbooks that needs consideration; the way in which such texts are used and the way in which they function in schools needs also to be considered. Consequently while we need to know something of what constitutes a particular text, we also need to know what happens to it in the classroom.

To explore issues such as these, something needs to be known of the dominant pedagogical discourses which inform language and literature education, the currently acceptable approaches to reading, writing and working with texts. Much of the important work associated with language, gender and schooling has, in the past, not directly addressed these discourses. It has instead, and understandably so, focussed upon the tangible linguistic evidence of inequality—upon teacher–student interaction (Spender and Sarah, 1980; Swann and Graddol, 1988); upon curriculum issues (Sheridan, 1982; Stacey et al., 1974; Whyte et al., 1985); and upon stereotypical family, student, and teacher expectations (Clarricoates, 1978; Connell et al., 1982; Stanworth, 1984). All of these areas have their own sets of tensions and unresolved ambiguities, as work by Valerie Walkerdine (1984), Rob Gilbert (1989) and R.W. Connell (1987) demonstrates in different ways. However, all three areas have made important contributions to mapping the terrain, and all need to be reconsidered here in a chapter which frames the pedagogical construction of femininity.

Consequently this chapter will initially review some of what has become widely known about language practices in the classroom from early work on sexism, bias and stereotyping in texts and teacher talk. It will then consider what might now be learnt from the features of the dominant discourses on language and literary education which could add new and helpful perspectives to classroom practices, and perhaps indicate how challenges to these discourses exist in competing fields of contemporary studies. Issues that consequently seem to be of key importance in the nexus between popular cultural texts, girls and language classrooms will form the last section of this chapter.

Sexism in the classroom

The importance that school language practices might play in the construction of gender identities for children has generally been seen to lie within three domains: in the nature and selection of curriculum materials; in teachers' classroom interactions with girls and boys; and in the expectations made of girls and boys by teachers, librarians, principals, parents and so on. Whatever texts are introduced into classrooms—be they the popular contemporary texts of a consumer culture, or the elitist classical texts of a literary culture—it is reasonable to assume that these three issues need to be considered.

Sexism in classroom texts

Over the past twenty years or so, the content of children's curriculum materials—reading textbooks and kits, children's picture books, and award-winning children's literature texts—has been steadily scrutinised in terms of gender portrayals for children. As we noted in chapter 1, the results are as would be expected. Almost without exception, such books and kits appear to present limited and unrealistic portrayals of women and girls, and despite concern expressed by educators, and the release of non-sexist guidelines by a number of publishing houses, the situation seems not to have altered significantly in contemporary times.

Reading schemes—materials typically used as compulsory, daily reading material in the first few years of school—have been regarded as main offenders (Children's Rights Workshop, 1976; Luke, 1988), and recently in Australia there have been several studies of the bias of local, and often contemporary, kits. For instance, a study by Jonathon Anderson and Lyn Yip (1987), comparing the content of two editions of a popular and well-used Australian reading scheme (one edition published in 1966, and the other in 1980), concluded that a recent publishing date did not necessarily indicate enlightened content. While the research indicated that the more modern readers did increase the presentation of occupational roles for women from two (1966) to three (1980), the corresponding increase for men was from eight (1966) to nineteen (1980). The 1980s version of this scheme had apparently not broken away from gender stereotyping, and the researchers concluded that both editions were biased and discriminatory.

The general trend noted in Anderson and Yip's discussion

of the content of school reading kits can be supported by the results of a much larger and rather different study by Peter Freebody and Carolyn Baker (1987). Freebody and Baker analysed 84000 words of text from 163 early reading books published recently by major publishing houses in Australia. By using word counts, word relationship configurations, and conversational exchange structure analysis, they were able to comment upon a number of more subtle features of gender-stereotyping than content analysis would normally produce. Typical findings were that, in these readers, 'boy/s' appears more frequently than 'girl/s' by a ratio of about three to two; that boys are more likely than girls to appear as single (i.e., individual) characters; that a much wider range of verbs is associated with boys than with girls; that use of the adjective 'little' is most frequently associated with girls, as is use of the verbs 'hold on to', and 'kiss', and the adjectives 'young', 'dancing', and 'pretty'.

In addition, Freebody and Baker detailed the stereotyped nature of adult and child behaviour portrayed in the readers. They found that it was fathers who 'paint', 'pump', 'fix', 'drive' (car), 'pull', 'start' (car), 'water' (garden), 'light' (fire), 'milk' (cow), 'shout', 'let', 'keep'. By comparison, it is mothers who 'bake', 'dress', 'hug', 'kiss' (a child), 'pack', 'pick' (flowers), 'set' (the table), 'splash', and 'thank'. In the same vein, it is the girls in these readers who 'love'—often and indiscriminately. Girls in school readers love not only humans, but also pets, nature, and selected objects. By comparison the only reference Freebody and Baker found to a boy loving anything was in the statement that Jack loved his horse.

It would seem that reading kits are no different from most other texts which have been written especially for children. Similar stereotypical pictures have emerged in studies of children's literature, many of which have focussed on groups of bookaward winners as identifiable, and presumably representative and highly acclaimed sets of texts. For instance Stephanie Reeder's study (1981) of the Australian Children's Book of the Year Award winners from 1950 to 1980 is a typical example of work of this nature. Reeder examined the role models presented in these texts 'to ascertain whether sex-role stereotyping in Australian children's books was a subject for historical study or was still a matter for contemporary concern' (p. 11). She hypothesised that the role models in the books would surely reflect the changing social patterns from 1950 to 1980, but her overall conclusion was that:

... the literature chosen as representative of the best in Australian children's books does not fully reflect the social development of the last thirty years with regard to sex-roles... males were numerically more represented than females; the roles represented were mostly in accordance with traditional role models... and occupational and family roles were limited to restrictions based on sex rather than individual differences, abilities or interests. (Reeder, 1981: p. 15)

Studies of picture story books commonly chosen for early literacy classrooms in Australian schools (Mortimer and Bradley, 1979) still support this general trend, although there are undoubtedly more contemporary books to feel positive about, as indicated by a recent study of American Caldecott winners and 'honor books' between 1981 and 1985 (Dougherty and Engel, 1987). Research at all levels of schooling, however, consistently indicates that material used to teach reading and writing at any age level is still surprisingly stereotyped and narrow in its portrayal of sex roles (see Gilbert, 1989a).

Talking at school

The effect that such book bias might have is intensified by the well documented research of the past twenty years on the different ways in which teachers talk to boys and girls in classrooms. In an era which has acknowledged the value of talking to learn (Barnes et al., 1971) and of the role that language plays in education (the Bullock Report, 1974), inequalities of classroom talk have been seen seriously to disadvantage girls (Schools Commission, 1975). Substantial work on the discriminatory nature of current English usage, and on the differences between the ways in which women and men speak to each other (see, for example, Thorne et al., 1983) is also well documented, and the impact of these broader social patterns of speech on classrooms has been generally acknowledged (Spender, 1980; Poynton, 1985; Baker and Davies, 1989).

The evidence of classroom language research over the past twenty years has made it clear that schoolgirls in mixed classrooms—and in fact women in any mixed educational institution—are seriously disadvantaged in both the quantity and quality of classroom interactions or speaking positions that are readily accessible to them. For whatever reasons, girls do not talk in lessons as much as boys do (Sears and Feldman, 1974; French and French, 1984), and when they are given turns to talk, the form of answers they are encouraged to give are frequently in the form of 'closed', short answers (Fichtelius et al., 1980). This appears to be in direct contrast to teacher questioning of boys, where 'open-ended' questions are more frequently asked.

Instead talking in class appears to be regarded as a male prerogative (Spender, 1980), with teachers valuing and urging male participation, and giving non-verbal indicators to boys through direction and timing of eye contact, to signal support for them to answer and lead class discussion (Swann and Graddol, 1988). Research on classroom talk has concluded that predictable patterns of female students' silence, passivity and withdrawal at school can be linked, at least in part, to various discriminatory patterns of teacher talk (Poynton, 1985).

Stereotypical expectations

Such patterns of teacher talk seem typical of a much broader problem: stereotypical teacher—and societal—expectations of female students. Michelle Stanworth's research (1984) provides one of the clearest demonstrations of teacher stereotyping, but several other studies (Stacey et al., 1974; Clarricoates, 1978; Spender and Sarah, 1980; Connell et al., 1982; and Culley and Portugues, 1985) provide similar evidence. Teachers not only choose classroom materials that are more suitable for boys, but they seem to have higher expectations of boys' potential, enjoy teaching boys more, and spend more classroom time with boys. As Katherine Clarricoates notes from her primary school research:

> The teachers' cultural expectations guided the behaviour of their pupils...girls' real ability is attributed to conformity to institutional expectations, and...the academic achievement of girls in schools is explained in terms of the feminine stereotype. The girls' conscientiousness and diligence makes them 'less bothersome' and 'less interesting' to the teachers...(Clarricoates, 1978: p. 359)

But to put the 'problem' as simply as this is perhaps to miss the most damaging stereotyping of all. Qualities of speech, forms of knowledge and patterns of behaviour regarded as typical of women have consistently been devalued or ignored. The almost unthinking support given by schools to 'man-made' history, sport, literature, and science is compatible with so-cietal support for such endeavours (Spender, 1980, 1982) and classroom language practices are the linguistic and social evidence of such patriarchal societal systems at work. Most of the research on children's books and curriculum matter, on classroom interaction, and on stereotypical expectations of girls, provides consistent evidence to that effect.

Teaching about texts

However, there is another aspect to classroom language practices which has not often been considered as significant, yet which is of primary importance when we wish to consider the relationships between popular cultural texts and the classroom. How do schools teach about texts, about reading, about writing? And which texts are likely to be valued and selected for classroom use?

Language and language learning

Since the 1960s, the dominant pedagogy associated with classroom language teaching has been one which emphasises the personal, expressive and imaginative potential of language: a pedagogy which has focussed on personal growth through language learning, and the power of self-expression (Allen, 1980; Gilbert, 1989b). Such an approach to language and language learning was first given a firm theoretical frame with the publication of John Dixon's *Growth Through English* in 1967, but it was very compatible with the creative writing movement of the 1960s (e.g., Langdon, 1961), and is perhaps typified by statements like this by a member of a well known British writing research team in the early 1970s: '. . .I should want . . .to merge the image of the writer in an image of the individual—as a person committed to his (sic) own search for meaning, who has to interpret the flow of events which happen to him and re-interpret in his own way the wisdom and knowledge of others which lies outside him, as a person. . .' (Burgess et al., 1973: p. 23)

Claims like these later became the basis for the language and learning guides of the early 1970s (Barnes et al., 1971), and for the argument that language learning was personal and individualistic. Not surprisingly, in the 1970s and 1980s learning to write and to read have frequently been described as expressive and naturalistic processes. For instance, Donald Graves— a leading American exponent of the process approach to writing—claims that 'writing, real writing, is exposure of inmost thoughts and feelings' (in Walshe, 1981: p. 8).

Discourses like these rely on a number of key words which establish a clear dichotomy between the 'good' language classroom and the 'bad'. In the good classroom language learning is natural, personal, individual, spontaneous, truthful, involved, emotional, real, whereas in the bad classroom language is associated with the unnatural, the impersonal, the premeditated, the contrived, the artificial. Holding this dichotomy together is the metaphor of 'personal voice' (Gilbert, 1989b), a metaphor which Derrida would argue (1976) ties the discourse to a human voice as the ultimate essence and source of meaning.

According to the practitioner guides, successful language learning is about finding your own 'personal voice', and teachers are advised to listen for these individual 'voices'. One writing practitioner writes: 'The student, in his (sic) writing, is speaking. The student with his own tone of voice rises off the page...enough to reveal his whole attitude, his point of view, his tone of voice' (Murray, 1982: p. 153).

These assumptions about language also underlie the currently popular whole language movement, which has been particularly significant in the development of a number of major and expensive curriculum initiatives in North America and Australia. The 'writing as process' approach in North America, and the Early Literacy In-Service Course (ELIC) in Australia have both derived largely from the traditions of naturalism and individualism as outlined above, and both have spread significantly throughout the USA, Canada, the UK, Australia and New Zealand.

The emphasis on a whole person and on a whole language has obvious pedagogical value and professional appeal to teachers. Professionally and pedagogically such concepts are compatible with contemporary moves towards integrating the curriculum and towards humanising and personalising schooling. They are also compatible with the more recent empowering concepts popularised in American language journals (Ashcroft, 1987). But the persistent—and at times insistent—emphasis on the personal and the individual in discussions of language learning, has tended to obscure the socially constructed nature of language practices. Instead of focussing on the social aspects of learning to talk, to listen, to read and to write, the focus has been upon the personal, individual, and wholistic nature of learning language.

Not surprisingly, this has had an important influence on pedagogical awareness of gender issues in the language classroom. A recent Australian evaluation of ELIC (Luke et al., 1990) noted how firmly the course was rooted in naturalism and individualism, and how effectively this ruled out debate on the social and cultural nature of language learning. According to this recent evaluation report, issues of gender, race and class were not seen to be relevant issues in early literacy classrooms working from within the ELIC framework.

Indeed research which has sought to address ideological issues such as these has often been marginalised from the dominant pedagogical discourses. As has been argued elsewhere (Willinsky, 1987; Kress, 1988; Gilbert, 1989b; Luke and Baker, 1990), criticism of the personal growth and process approaches to language learning—particularly in terms of learning to read and write—has not been welcomed or valued, and can not, of course, be readily accommodated within the dominant discourses. The result has been that a consideration of the way in which language practices contribute towards the construction of gendered identities has been rather noticeably absent from the discussion. Language, when regarded as the natural ebb and flow of day-to-day existence, is too easily regarded as a neutral message system: an almost transparent system through which teachers and students communicate.

Reading and textual analysis

Just as an emphasis on personalism and individualism has dominated practitioner guides to language learning, so too has it dominated approaches to the selection and study of classroom texts. This has been the result of significant shifts in literary theory over the past twenty years, shifts which have challenged the composition of an elite canon of acclaimed texts, the nature of academic literary criticism, and the source of textual meaning. Out of the upheaval that has occurred in literary theory, one field—reader-response criticism—has emerged as the most likely and popular contender for the classroom, largely because of its compatibility with many of the tenets of the 1970s approaches to language and learning as outlined earlier (see Gilbert, 1987).

Reader-oriented aesthetics has now become increasingly popular in school discourses about texts and about reading (Jackson, 1980; Corcoran and Evans, 1987), taking its cue from the work of theorists like Louise Rosenblatt, who claims, 'Every time a reader experiences a work of art, it is in a sense created anew. Fundamentally, the process of understanding a work implies a recreation of it, an attempt to grasp completely the structured sensations and concepts through which the author seeks to convey the quality of his (sic) sense of life' (Rosenblatt, 1976: p. 113) The concept of textual meaning lying in the reader's hands—in this case the student's hands—is clearly compatible with similar moves in language education in the 1970s and 1980s. It is the individual and personal response to a text which is seen to be important, not the way in which that response is class and gender-specific, nor the ideological nature of the text's social construction and commercial production. By shifting a focus to individual response to texts, discourses like this again emphasise the apparent neutrality and innocence of language as a simple connecting line between two points of consciousness: the author and the reader. The focus is on emotional response, not on what constitutes an emotional response, nor on how particular reading practices make such responses possible and likely.

This shift in focus to reader-response aesthetics has been partially responsible for a number of important shifts in recent times. Theories which seem to be claiming the death of the single authoritative reading of a text—formerly the domain of literary criticism and associated in many teachers' eyes with the elitism of literary study—offer relief to teachers who have long struggled with the traditional work of unravelling texts' hidden meanings. At last student meanings, in all their naivety, tentativeness, insufficiency and perhaps outright misinterpretation can be taken aboard as legitimate because they represent personal engagements with texts.

If readers create meanings individually and personally, then—the argument goes—all students have equal rights to create their own meanings. No one student's meaning is necessarily any better than another's. We all have rights to our own responses, as long as they are personally ours and genuinely felt. Indeed the only guiding principle for a 'good response' seems to be that it should be a personal one, one felt deeply and emotionally by the student.

The actual ways in which students might respond to a text can, however, vary, and response aesthetics does offer a host of possibilities for classroom practice. Texts become the common content from which to launch a thousand and one different language activities. And yet the content, as Freebody and Baker (1987) notice in their study of the content of children's basal readers, is really seen to be irrelevant: it is quite 'idle'. It has been subsumed by the larger goal of instruction in language. What children read about—and then what they will write and talk about—seems to be of minor concern. The content of classroom books has thus almost incidentally become the content for classroom language activities.

As a further example of this, many early literacy classrooms now use literature texts as the preferred reading instruction material, a move endorsed by programmes such as ELIC and the Shared Book Experience approach. It is commonly argued that it is good classroom practice to use real books for the teaching of reading. As Denise Ryan writes in the Foreword to Terry Johnson and Daphne Louis's very popular and internationally well known *Literacy through Literature*: 'In recent years teachers have turned more and more to children's literature to form the basis of their classroom language program. They have recognised the importance of children reading literature that is accessible in language and meaning, literature that "speaks to them"' (Ryan in Johnson and Louis, 1985: p. 9).

Literature seems to offer something of the same honesty, spontaneity, naturalness, authenticity and personalism so sought in children's writing, and as such is directly compared to the artificially constructed, unnatural, inauthentic and impersonal basal reader texts of early periods, and directly linked with enjoyment in reading. Literary texts are real texts. And the definition of a *real* text has now become very broadly based. Populist children's authors like Roald Dahl are immensely successful in primary schools in Australia, and the rising fortunes of school book clubs (see Willinsky and Hunniford, 1986) have given series like *Choose Your Own Adventure* and *The Babysitters' Club* large commercial markets of schoolchildren. Secondary school students are similarly accustomed to best-selling thrillers, romances, detection and science fiction novels being adopted within the English classroom.

The interesting question, however, is how gender relations are dealt with in the more popular—the more 'real'—cultural texts. Studies of best-selling popular texts (see, for instance, Eco, 1978; Carr, 1989; Fiske, 1989) suggest that the dominant reading positions constructed in such formulaic fiction rely extensively on stereotypical versions of femininity and masculinity, and in Part II of this book we consider some of these claims.

Working with texts

Classrooms are never sites of unified and coherent meanings, and while it could well be argued that certain discourses dominate in the practitioner guides for the classroom, they often maintain a fragile hold within classroom walls. While teachers might well wish to construct classrooms where communities of writers and readers work co-operatively and imaginatively together to construct personally satisfying texts, the realities of classrooms are often those of assessment and evaluation; of grading, sorting and ranking; of disciplining, punishing and controlling; of sexual and racial harassment.

Within classrooms there are also a number of alternative discourses which challenge—and occasionally support—the dominant understandings of language and of language study. In this chapter we will briefly consider the contribution that several of these might make to understandings of the relationship between schools, popular cultural texts, and the construction of gendered subjectivity. The impact of genre theory, feminist theories of writing and of literature, and theories of language, ideology and subjectivity, all seem to offer potentially different perspectives for the concerns of this book.

Genre and school language study: natural or learned

Not surprisingly, one of the most serious challenges to the argument that language learning is natural, personal and creative has come from sociolinguistics. In Australia, a team of researchers working loosely within a systemic-linguistic framework advocated by Michael Halliday, has played a significant role in focussing attention upon the conventions of particular written and spoken genres. The work of Gunther Kress (1982), Frances Christie (1984), and Jim Martin (1985) has laid out some of the sociolinguistic parameters of common school language activities, and by so doing, has emphasised the learned social patterns that make such activities recognisable, readable, repeatable. Whether or not teachers should actively teach some of these language patterns or genres to children has become the hub of the debate, and was given form in a collection of papers edited by Ian Reid—*The Place of Genre in Learning: Current Debates* (1987).

The papers in Reid's volume can be loosely sorted into two main philosophical camps. On one hand the process and personal growth advocates condemn the potential rigidity and narrowness of generic convention; on the other linguists claim that it is dishonest and inequitable not to make knowledge of language and language systems available to all children. This latter position is typified by Christie's statement that:

An educational process in an important sense is a process of initiation: an initiation, that is, into the ways of working, or of behaving, or of thinking...particular to one's cultural traditions. Mastery of these ways of working, which are necessarily encoded very heavily in linguistic patternings, represents mastery of the capacity to exercise choice: choice that is to say, in that one is empowered to make many kinds of meanings, enabled to operate with confidence in one's world...Learning the genres of one's culture is both part of entering into it with understanding, and part of developing the necessary ability to change it. (Christie, 1987: p. 30)

However, as Bill Green (1987) points out in a chapter in the same volume, the generic approach's potential both for power and for rigidity has important implications for gender. His claim is that the genre position could be interpreted as 'a complicity in the cultural task of schooling'; as 'a means of (re)producing the dominant hegemonic culture, including the 'proper' order of gendered identities and relations' (p. 86). Green cites Jacques Derrida's warning: 'As soon as the word "genre" is sounded, as soon as it is heard, as soon as one attempts to conceive it, a limit is drawn. And when a limit is drawn, norms and interdictions are not far behind' (in Green, 1987: p. 87).

The possible rigidity of the genre position is also taken up by Anne Freadman (1987) in the last chapter in Reid's volume. Freadman's argument is that while genre is undoubtedly a key concept in the theory of discourse, and an informing concept in the constitution and processing of texts, it is not only a linguistic concept. Her argument is that it is *time* and *place* which constitute and mark out a particular genre.

Where a particular text occurs, and *when* it does, have important implications for the nature of various genres. A romance in a feminist journal will be different from one in *Playboy* or *The Women's Weekly*, and similarly romances of the late twentieth century are rather different from those of the late nineteenth: they arise out of, and are constructed by, different discourses. Consequently the *site* of a particular text—where and when it occurs—helps to position the reader in what Freadman calls, 'the right game' (1987: p. 21). It helps readers to position themselves in expectation of particular genres and particular texts. It thus becomes a crucial factor to take into consideration when assessing how girls and young women are positioned as subjects within certain discourses. As we will discuss in Part II of this book, the genre of the teen romance novel cannot be properly understood outside its connection with other systems which similarly position women. The genres typical of television soap operas work in the same way.

Genres cannot then only be seen as sets of identifiable linguistic conventions. While it is important, for instance, to recognise the conventions of a fairy tale, it is more important to know how such conventions vary, dependent upon the discourses within which they are sited, and from within which they were produced. Jack Zipes' social historical analysis of *The Trials and Tribulations of Little Red Riding Hood* (1983a) is a good example of this variability, as he demonstrates how different versions of the folk tale of Red Riding Hood have been produced at different times, to serve different cultural purposes. The main changes that Zipes details are changes in the construction of the central female character, changes that see Red Riding Hood alter from a wily, strong folk heroine to a passive, foolish victim of male lust.

Bronwyn Mellor's teaching guides, *Reading Stories* (1987) and *Reading Hamlet* (1989), are similarly powerful in the way they shed light on the constructed nature of reading. Mellor demonstrates how it is possible to read stories differently, dependent upon the position the reader takes up in relation to the text. However different readings are not seen to be purely idiosyncratic. Different readings of a text are instead seen to demonstrate how readers have different discursive histories. Such histories make it likely that readers will take up different reading positions or stances in relation to different texts, and then proceed to apply different reading practices or methods in their attempts to find order, meaning and purpose in various texts. As examples of this, both Zipes and Mellor demonstrate the cultural arbitrariness of reading and the danger of attributing fixed generic conventions to texts without taking time and place—the cultural site of a text—into account. In particular, different 'readings' make it possible to consider gender relations within texts, and it is here that a consideration of feminist aesthetics can be valuable.

Writing as a woman, reading as a woman

Just as genre theory challenges dominant pedagogical assumptions about the naturalness of language and language learning, feminist literary theory offers a challenge to dominant pedagogical assumptions about the nature of literature and literary response. Feminist literary theory has opened up for debate the question of literary truth, of the universality of the literary experience, and of the ways in which literature is produced.

It is impossible to speak of feminist literary theory as one field, as Toril Moi's *Sexual/Textual Politics* (1985) demonstrates.

Different questions have been asked at different times, by different groups of women and one of the noticeable features of current feminist theory is its eclecticism and willingness to incorporate a variety of critical approaches. For instance questions about the nature of woman writer and woman reader have been answered differently, dependent upon decisions to seek answers in psychoanalysis (Jacobus, 1986), in the female body (Irigaray, 1985), in mothering (Chodorow, 1978), or in theories of language and discourse (Weedon, 1987).

Sydney Kaplan (1985) claims that feminist literary criticism first had its origins in the personal responses women readers made to women writers, and in the implicit repudiation of any critical stance which claimed to be objective. She traces several varieties of criticism: revisionary criticism of the canon of great works, as with Judith Fetterley (1978); the study of neglected or lost women writers, as in the work of Sandra Gilbert and Susan Gubar (1979); and the articulation of a distinctive female literary tradition, as typified by the research of Elaine Showalter (1977). Noticeable in the early development of distinctively feminist aesthetics has been an emphasis on the value of a personal, female perspective, and a rejection of what had come to be regarded as a masculinist discourse of objective literary criticism. And for many women this had come to be associated with a growing awareness of feminism. As Kaplan writes:

> Like those of many other feminist critics, my personal motivations and my own personal history were beginning to merge with those of a powerful women's movement. . . Not only did many of us feel alienated by the content of the canon we were expected to 'master', but we also felt excluded by the assumed objectivity of the critical jargon we were expected to use, with its accompanying assumption of the generically masculine 'reader', its implied universality, as well as its estrangement from our lived experience. (Kaplan, 1985: p. 39)

Feminism had given women a speaking position of confidence and authority, and this placed them differently in traditional literary discourse. As a result those readers inscribed by feminist theory read the critical tradition in literature—and the canon of works it sought to promote—as a patriarchal tradition reinforcing images of character and behaviour which encouraged women to accept subordination. In other words, literary history was seen to have worked hand in glove with dominant patriarchal ideology. It had canonised certain texts which claimed to embody universal human truths and silenced those which interrogated or undermined those truths.

By seeking to expose this collusion and to open out the gaps and silences in literary traditions, feminist criticism offers itself as a political practice which radically redefines the nature of what counts as literature, and what counts as reading. In this way women's writing can often be read as both a simultaneous acceptance and rejection of the society that produced it: an acceptance of the forms or genres given, for example, but a rejection of the gendered and subordinate position such genres proffer. Thea Astley, one of Australia's foremost women writers, had this to say about the speaking space offered her as a young writer:

> ...I grew up in an era when women weren't supposed to have any thoughts at all, and if they did express thoughts then either no attention was paid to them or they were considered brash and aggressive. I also grew up in an era where they talked about 'women's' literature. 'It's a *woman's* book' they'd say, as if there was something wrong with that. So when I was eighteen or nineteen I thought to myself that the only way one could have any sort of validity was to write as a male...(in Baker, 1986: p. 42)

Astley's claim that she could choose to write as a male leads into the third of the adjacent fields which have challenged much of contemporary classroom lore about working with texts. What space is there for unravelling the complexities and limitations of learned gendered writing positions, and learned gendered reading positions, in a discourse driven by naturalism and personalism? Theories of textuality, discourse and subjectivity, dealing as they do with the constructed nature of reading and writing positions, would seem to offer more space and more possibilities for exploring the nature of such practices.

Language and subjectivity

The argument this book makes throughout is that the construction of the cultural text—both in its reading and its writing—is a learned social practice. It is not necessarily a natural or personal expression of emotion, although the conventions of many cultural texts serve to construct an illusion of naturalism, personalism and individual expression. Cultural texts—both in and out of classrooms—can best be seen as discursive products, positing particular speaking positions, and therefore, as Chris Weedon (1987) warns, necessarily involved in the construction of gendered subjectivities. Weedon's argument is that the construction of a particular subject position (of subjectivity), inevitably means the acceptance of a gendered subjectivity:

> . . . even when we resist a particular subject position and the mode of subjectivity which it brings with it, we do so from the position of an alternative social definition of femininity. In patriarchal societies we cannot escape the implications of femininity. Everything we do signifies compliance or resistance to dominant norms of what it is to be a woman. (1987: pp. 86–7)

Discourse always requires a speaking position—a position from which authority is exercised—and a spoken subject, a person brought into existence through the exercise of this authority. Studying and working with texts in this way—using these understandings of the workings of discourse—seem essential for critical feminist pedagogy, for they make it possible to deconstruct the construction of the gendered subject, both as writer and as reader.

Writing can then not be seen as a natural and personal response of the self, but as a learned social discursive practice of a gendered subject. Writing is thus acknowledged to be about taking up a particular speaking position in a discourse, and of then bringing certain subject positions into existence. But how many speaking positions of authority are available to young teenage women? From what discourses can they speak with power? And what versions of feminine subjectivity are able to be—or are encouraged to be—constructed in classrooms? Similarly reading becomes much more than a personal and idiosyncratic process. It too is learned—as the reader learns alternative reading frames or practices. Different readings are not, however, the result of individual differences. Rather, different readings are the result of the application of different reading frames, which are the result of the identification of different reading positions—different subject positions within the discourse.

Clearly subjectivity is more readily recognisable and acceptable when the subject position offered is compatible with a number of other dominant and powerful discourses. As we will demonstrate in chapter 4, *Dolly Fiction* is produced and marketed hand in hand with *Dolly* magazine, and thus is clustered with the representation of fashionable teenage femininity that the magazine constructs. It is thus seen to be compatible with commercial consumer images of femininity marketed in teen cosmetics, perfumes, clothing, and music, and this compatibility thus significantly strengthens the power of the images constructed by making them seem natural, inevitable, and obvious.

As a result, what possibilities for resistance do young women have to these images of femininity, and how might resistance be supported and strengthened through the introduction of young women to alternative subject positions in alternative discourses? And what implications does this have for classrooms, in terms of the ways in which we would talk about readings and the construction of gendered identities through such readings? Part II and III of this book will begin to address these questions, by focussing on a series of case studies which consider a number of specific texts, and on the parameters of a possible feminist pedagogy. A television soap opera, a romance series, and girls' school essays will all be considered, with each chapter questioning the role these particular texts play in the construction of feminine subjectivity. As well, these chapters will address the tensions, contradictions and ambiguities that sometimes result when these popular cultural texts are intertwined with the textuality of the classroom.

Part II

Reading the texts

3

Days of their lives: watching the soaps

Subtly, in complicated ways, recognising some conflict and problems, discourses on female desire nevertheless work inexorably towards closure, towards putting the lid on love, desire and especially on change. (Coward, 1984: p. 16)

We begin our analyses of some cultural texts which are popular with girls and young women by examining television soap operas. We indicated in chapter 1 that popular cultural texts are significant in the reproduction and circulation of patriarchal gender ideologies, and as they are the most popular programmes with female television viewers, soap operas would seem to be an appropriate focus in the exploration of the role of popular cultural texts in the construction of femininity.

Soap operas are significant cultural texts in teenage girls' out of school lives. Understanding the place and meaning of soap operas in their lives is relevant to understanding how they make sense of themselves, and is important in thinking through more appropriate ways of working with this group in the classroom. As Rosalind Coward has written: 'As feminists we have to be constantly alerted to *what* reality is being constructed, and *how* representations are achieving this construction (1985: p. 227). As we outlined in chapter 1, we view representational cultural texts such as soap operas as closely interrelated with lived social relations. 'Reading' a cultural text can be seen as a kind of dialogue between the text and a socially situated reader. Furthermore, a particular television programme will be read in relation to other television programmes and advertisements, other cultural texts such as magazines and films, and also in the context of the everyday

47

social relations of the viewer. For example, a young woman who reads an issue of *Dolly* magazine will bring to bear the textual knowledge she has acquired based on her own social positioning, as well as knowledge from her previous experiences with *Dolly* and other magazines, books, films and television programmes.

So, although we have said that popular cultural texts are significant in the reproduction and circulation of patriarchal gender ideologies, they do not transmit such ideologies in a straightforward or simple way. A television programme can only be a *bearer* or *provoker* of meanings and pleasures, and as Fiske emphasises: 'An essential characteristic of television is its polysemy, or multiplicity of meanings. A program provides a potential of meanings which may be realised, or made into actually experienced meanings, by socially situated viewers in the process of reading' (1987: p. 16). Although television texts strongly promote dominant ideologies through their preferred readings, they will also contain contradictions and counter ideologies, and it is because of this multiplicity of meanings that a television programme can become popular with a wide range of groups.

This contradictory richness in popular programmes results from the tension for programme producers between the ideological content of a programme and the need to entertain. The constraints upon producers to create use-values associated with entertainment limits their ability to produce at the same time a commodity which promotes dominant ideologies. Consequently, as Terry Lovell argues, 'ideological production always occurs under contradictory pressures, and...its results are therefore never, or rarely, ideologically consistent and uni-dimensional' (1981: p. 47).

This is significant in relation to the *consumers* of a programme, as viewers 'will only produce meanings from, and find pleasures in, a television program if it allows for an articulation of their interests' (Fiske, 1987: p. 83). The accumulation of experiences and knowledge of subordinated groups, and the strategies by which they respond to their position of subordination is required for people to make pleasurable meanings from popular cultural forms. Hence the meanings made may not only be oppositional to the preferred dominant ideologies which may be strongly promoted in a television text, but will validate the social experiences of subordinate groups. The political significance of such validation is problematic: is such validation a radical first step towards empowerment of subordinate groups or does it merely ensure acceptance of their social situation? We will return to this point later in the chapter.

Valerie Walkerdine's perceptive study (1986) of a working-class English family watching *Rocky II* on video illustrates our argument concerning the way viewers relate to popular cultural texts. Walkerdine explores the activity of watching the video in relation to the class and gender dynamics within the family, and also explores the links between the fantasy space of the film and the viewers. She is particularly interested in the meaning for Mr Cole, the father of the family, of the boxing sequences in the video, which he repeatedly replays. According to Walkerdine, fighting, as a key signifier in the film, is related to a class-specific as well as gendered lived experience. She argues that although fighting may be seen by some analysts as representing a particularly 'macho' version of masculinity, the fantasy of the fighter is the fantasy of the working-class male and must be seen in this context. For Mr Cole, fighting 'is a key term in a discourse of powerlessness, of a constant struggle not to sink, to get rights, not to be pushed out' (Walkerdine, 1986: p. 182).

In this way television viewers make sense of programmes in terms of their own social positioning. While a popular cultural text such as a television programme is a single commodity in the financial economy, in the *cultural economy* it provides a *repertoire* of meanings (Fiske, 1987). In the context of our concerns about meanings and gender we are interested in the repertoires which are offered by soap operas. In other words, what versions of femininity are offered by soap opera texts and what is made of them by viewers?

In this chapter we provide a brief account of the history of 'the soaps', and review research on women and soap operas and girls and television viewing. We then report a case study of soap opera viewing among teenage girls and discuss a particular soap opera popular with this group. In the final section of the chapter we draw some implications about the role of soap operas in the construction of femininity in girls and young women, and the potential of such cultural texts for challenging dominant gender ideologies.

Never-ending stories

Soap operas were first developed for radio in the 1930s, though the serial form had been used in magazines for many years to boost circulation. For example, the first movie serial produced in the USA, *What Happened to Mary*, was based on such a magazine serial. Radio serials and later soap operas developed from these initial serialisations. Daytime radio serials, which were sponsored by soap companies, rapidly became extremely successful with radio audiences, and came to be known as 'soap operas'. Within ten years after the first television soap had been produced in the USA, television had become the dominant soap opera medium (Mayer, 1989).

In Australia, as in the USA, a large number of radio serials were initially developed, and these were subsequently followed by television soap operas. The first Australian soap was *Bellbird* in 1967, but by the 1980s several Australian soaps were screened in the early evening (Mayer, 1989). While daytime soap operas shown on Australian television are still mainly from the USA, most of the prime-time soaps are Australian and are targetted for family audiences. Both types of soap opera share the same general characteristics, though settings in prime-time soaps, such as *Neighbours* and *Home and Away*, tend to be less opulent than those in daytime soaps, and the world portrayed tends to be of urban and semi-urban middle-class Australia (Mayer, 1989: p. 14).

The term 'soap opera', with its linking of commercialism with a 'high' art form, had perjorative overtones from its inception (Mayer, 1989), and these overtones have not disappeared: 'If television is considered by some to be a vast wasteland, soap operas are thought to be the least nourishing spot in the desert. The surest way to damn a film, a television programme, or even a situation in real life is to invoke an analogy to soap operas' (Modleski, 1982: p. 86). And Charlotte Brunsdon (1986) similarly notes that soap opera fans are denigrated by both 'quality' and popular newspapers, and even those involved in the production of soap operas are often apologetic about their product. Such negative views about soap operas are clearly related to the fact that the programmes are particularly targeted for and popular with women. Other popular cultural texts, for example action series, are rarely criticised in such disparaging terms, and we would argue that the dismissal of soap opera as 'trash' is part of the general devaluing of women's culture and interests within patriarchy.

The characteristics of the soap opera genre have been discussed by a number of writers in recent years. For example, based on her Australian study of women and soap operas,

Mary Ellen Brown (1987: p. 4) identifies eight characteristics of soap opera texts as follows:

1 serial form which resists narrative closure;
2 multiple characters and plots;
3 use of time which parallels actual time and implies that the action takes place whether we watch it or not;
4 abrupt segmentation between parts;
5 emphasis on dialogue, problem solving, and intimate conversation;
6 many of the male characters portrayed as 'sensitive men';
7 female characters often professional or otherwise powerful in the world outside the home;
8 the home, or some other place which functions as a home, is the setting for the show.

Some of these characteristics will be discussed in more detail later in the chapter, but the first two relate to the issue of open texts which we have discussed previously. In contrast to traditional narrative forms which have a beginning, a middle, and an ending, soap opera texts work through an extended middle section. And while individual plots may end, there is no overall sense of finality. Thus we have in effect a *never-ending story*: a story with a constant sense of irresolution. As Fiske puts it: 'This infinitely extended middle means that soap operas are never in a state of equilibrium... their world is one of perpetual disturbance and threat' (1987: p. 180).

Of course, the serial form of soap operas is important in constructing a regular audience, and Brown (1987) reports that for this reason daytime soaps are extremely profitable for producers because they attract large audiences of women and can be produced cheaply. They also provide a readily targetable audience for advertising. The relationship between the soap opera and the advertisements which accompany it is of interest. Modleski argues that one of the more obvious contradictions of the soap opera screening is that the two views of domestic life presented via the soaps and the advertising that accompanies them are antithetical. She argues that both daytime commercials and soap operas are set in the home, and yet housework, washing and cooking, the major focus of the advertisements that are screened with soaps, is a focus which is excluded from the soap operas themselves (1982: p. 101). Other writers, for example John Tulloch (1989), have emphasised that there is both continuity and antithesis in the 'flow' of soaps and advertisements. We will discuss this point further later in the chapter.

Soaps as cultural texts

Despite being fairly universally damned as 'trash', soap operas have received a good deal of attention from writers interested in the appeal they hold for women and their value in terms of feminist politics. Some feminist critics, for example, have been interested in the emphasis in soap opera texts on devalued aspects of women's culture (e.g., Brunsdon, 1986), while others argue that they help women to accept their position within patriarchal society (e.g., Modleski, 1982). Most of the research undertaken has focussed on the characteristics of the genre and on the discourses transmitted, and in this section we will consider some of these analyses.

Charlotte Brunsdon (1981) argues that soap operas are relevant to women because they focus on personal problems—particularly those relating to birth, marriage, divorce and death—within a family setting. She argues that even when outside events are included, they are dealt with from the point of view of the personal, and that the open multiple-plotted structure of soap operas allows for greater audience involvement with the personal lives of the characters. In fact it seems that the pleasure of soap operas for women lies in the ongoing personal involvement which the cyclical nature of the programmes allows.

This is a position also adopted by Tanya Modleski, who argues that soap operas provide a unique narrative feminine form of pleasure which 'has become thoroughly adapted to the rhythms of women's lives in the home...' (1982, p. 87). However, Modleski's analysis is more critical in terms of the outcomes of this pleasure. She suggests that the endless deferment which characterises soap operas, and the associated focus on processes rather than outcomes, makes the anticipation of an end in itself, and argues that this teaches women to forgo the satisfaction of their desires in favour of minor pleasures. Modleski also argues that soap operas teach women to 'read' people and to be sensitive to their feelings, firstly by encouraging viewers to identify with the characters, and secondly by using close-ups and 'holding' shots to heighten emotional reaction. Soap operas may also offer assurance of the immortality of the family even though it is portrayed in constant turmoil (Modleski, 1982). The danger of soaps for Modleski is that they allay 'real needs' and 'real desires' through a fantasy world: 'The isolation, solitude, and drudgery of the housewife's world are denied in the creation of a very different world: "Another World"' (1982: p. 112).

An additional aspect of a consideration of soap operas as cultural texts relates to sexuality. Modleski (1982) views soaps as mirroring the role of women under patriarchy, with identity being dependent on relationships with husband and children, and with women continually having to accommodate to changes in these relationships. Other writers, however, for example Mary Ellen Brown (1987), argue that soaps show women in powerful relationships with men, and portray a view of sexuality which focusses on relationships and feelings rather than on the body. She suggests that soap opera texts portray a more nurturant version of masculinity than is seen in other series, and that more 'macho' characteristics tend to be reserved for the 'villain' in soaps. According to Brown then, soaps are positive and empowering in the way that they handle sexual pleasure; sexuality is seen either as a positive source of pleasure or as a means of empowerment in a male-dominated world.

However, as we have argued previously, representational cultural texts are closely interrelated with lived social relations, and analyses of cultural texts are of little value unless there is also a consideration of how the texts are used in women's lives and how meanings are made of them. In addition, there is a tendency to over-generalise in such analyses and to fail to take account of the differences between daytime and prime-time soaps, and also of the characteristics of *particular* soaps. Much more useful in our view is research, such as Ien Ang's (1985), which attempts to take account of the complex relationship between text, readers and their social situation.

Ang's (1985) research focussed on how women viewers *experience* soap operas—in particular how they experience watching *Dallas*. Her research, conducted in The Netherlands, was based on 42 letters which she received in response to an advertisement placed in a women's magazine asking for people to write to her about their reactions to *Dallas*. One significant aspect of the research was that Ang was interested in exploring the relationship between pleasure and ideology in the way in which this prime-time soap opera was experienced by this select group of viewers.

Ang claims that the melodramatic themes of soap opera

texts are as significant as their structural features in the construction of the 'tragic structure of feeling': the complex of meanings viewers can read from a soap opera. Structures of feeling, following Raymond Williams (1977), can be described as shared ways of seeing ourselves and the world, though as Ang emphasises, a structure of feeling is experienced at an emotional rather than a cognitive level. Ang's 'tragic structure of feeling' which is constructed by soaps is the idea that life is always full of 'ups and downs', that 'happiness can never last for ever but, quite the contrary, is precarious' (1985: p. 46).

Thus it is insight into the metaphorical value of the plot which is the basis of women's pleasure in soap opera viewing. Pleasure consists in the recognition of ideas that fit into the viewers' imaginative world: 'They can lose themselves in *Dallas* because the program symbolizes a structure of feeling which connects up with the ways they encounter life. And in so far as the imagination is an essential component of our psychological world, the pleasure of *Dallas*...is not a *compensation* for the presumed drabness of daily life, nor a *flight* from it, but a *dimension* of it' (Ang, 1985: p. 83).

Ang suggests that the field of tension between the fictional and the real plays an important part in the pleasure offered by watching *Dallas*. She writes that viewers identify with the emotional realism of the programme although there is a 'constant to-and-fro movement between identification with and distancing from the fictional world as constructed in the text' (1985: p. 50). It seems that the *practice* of soap opera viewing is important: women may become lost in the world of the programme as a kind of escape from the realities of daily life. Ang contends that in soap operas the contradictions of patriarchy are exposed and coped with at a fantasy level and that soaps allow women to 'bracket' reality for a while. She argues that involvement at this level can occur quite independently of their political position in 'real life', but does not reach a firm conclusion about whether soaps are progressive or conservative for women. Rather she suggests that fantasy and fiction operate independently from other aspects of women's lives. However, Brown (1987) sees soap opera viewing as having positive effects because at the same time as the myths of patriarchy are restructured in soap opera texts, a feminine culture is affirmed and legitimated. These views about the role of soap operas will be discussed further in the final section of this chapter.

Girls and television

In the context of our focus on the role of popular cultural texts in the lives of teenage girls, some previous Australian research findings are pertinent. Hodge and Tripp's (1986) research on schoolchildren and the soap opera *Prisoner* demonstrated the ways in which children were able to make sense of the programme in terms of their own experiences. In particular, the children drew parallels between life in prison and their lives at school. Other research (Thomas, 1980) found that *Prisoner* was used by working-class girls as a source of sub-cultural identity: the girls identified with the women prisoners and called their teachers 'the screws'. A further study by Patricia Palmer (1986a) found that Sydney schoolgirls similarly based their playground games on this programme. Research findings like these support the notion of an active audience, able to negotiate its own particular meanings from a cultural text, and are relevant to our earlier comments about the way people read cultural texts to affirm and articulate their own interests.

Palmer's (1986b) research on the role of television in the lives of 30 Sydney schoolgirls is particularly relevant to our exploration of the place and meaning of soap operas in the lives of teenage girls. Palmer found that the girls in her study expressed a strong preference for programmes, such as soap operas, with which they could become emotionally involved. The girls also expressed a preference for programmes which dealt with problems and everyday concerns of people their own age, and some even drew upon characters in the programme when thinking about themselves and their futures. The girls talked about television with their friends, and in fact there was evidence that particular friendship groups influenced programme 'favourites'. Palmer suggested also that in the case of some of the girls, certain programmes seemed to take on an added significance and became what she refers to as 'primers: texts for living' (1986b: pp. 56–8).

In the remaining sections of this chapter we present a case study of soap opera viewing among teenage girls which attempted to explore some of the questions raised by previous research (see also Taylor, 1989b). It seemed to be important to follow up Palmer's (1986b) suggestion that certain programmes may act as 'primers', and to ask to what extent soap operas might be described in this way for some girls, and in what ways they are related to the construction of femininity. Additionally, it seemed to be worthwhile to explore some of the

issues which have emerged from research such as that completed by Ang (1985) and Brown (1987) with adult soap opera
viewers. Of particular interest were two aspects highlighted by
their work: the relationship between 'reality' and fantasy, and
the relationship between pleasure and ideology.

Group interviews were conducted with students in two
Queensland state schools—one situated in a new working-
class area to the south of Brisbane (Southlands) and the other
in a middle-class suburb in Brisbane (Hillview). At Southlands
the interview group consisted of twelve girls (aged sixteen
to seventeen), and at Hillview eight girls (aged fourteen to
fifteen years) were interviewed. None of the students was
from an Aboriginal or migrant background.

The taped interviews were semi-structured, were conducted
informally with small friendship groups, and lasted for about
an hour. Questions ranged over programme likes and dislikes,
particularly in relation to opinions about soap operas. Students
were also asked about the extent to which soap opera viewing
was shared with family and friends, and at the end of the
interviews they were asked about other leisure interests and
their perceptions about their futures. The interviews, while
conducted in considerable depth, were based on a limited
sample of teenagers and therefore need to be seen as ex-
ploratory only. In the following discussion of the interview
material we will consider the girls' present lives and their
future plans, their views about soap operas, and the context
of their soap opera viewing.

Girls' lived experiences

The isolation and lack of leisure and community facilities for
young people in the Southlands area was regarded as a problem by the girls in this district. For example, going to the
movies entails a trip into Brisbane—usually by train as bus
services are infrequent—which adds substantially to the costs
involved in going out. The girls mentioned that there was
'nothing to do' in the local area, and, although several of them
had part-time jobs in local retail stores, cafes and fast-food
establishments (with two girls having two part-time jobs),
others had not been able to find jobs. This was partly due to
lack of employment opportunities in the area, but also due
to transport problems which prevented them from going
farther afield. Their employment opportunities were more
restricted than those of girls living closer to Brisbane, but they

are likely to be representative of large numbers of working-class girls in similar new outer suburban developments where unemployment levels are relatively high and many families are experiencing economic difficulties. At Hillview on the other hand girls were able to go out to movies and other entertainment in the city more easily. Those who were old enough had part-time jobs—either in the city or the local area.

When asked about their spare-time activities, most of the girls mentioned reading. Both novel and magazine reading were mentioned, and there were no significant differences in reading patterns between the girls from the two schools. Fantasies, mysteries, adventures and supernatural books were the most popular genres, although one girl said that she loved reading the *Sweet Dreams* and *Sweet Valley High* series romances. The most popular magazines were *Dolly*, *Countdown* and *Smash Hits*, though most girls also read *Woman's Weekly* and other women's magazines bought by other members of their families. Three of the Southlands girls read very little. One said that she read only magazines, one that she rarely read books, while another said that the only reading she did was 'the comics in the newspaper'.

The girls' other spare-time activities were varied. As most of their families owned video recorders, video watching was a common activity in both groups of girls, and video recording a regularly used convenience. Video recorders allowed girls to tape and watch their favourite programmes when they were unable to watch them at the scheduled time, and in some cases programmes were recorded on a regular basis. Other leisure activities included listening to the radio and taped music, or, in the case of the Southlands girls, going out to visit friends, 'sleeping over' at friends' houses and going to the shopping centre (for those for whom this was possible). Girls also went out with their families, and one girl commented that it was the only way she was able to go out at all. The only other spare-time interest mentioned—by two—was horse-riding, while some girls also mentioned previous interests, like ballet and skating, which they no longer pursued. The Hillview girls were more involved with hobbies and sports such as jazz ballet. This difference is probably a reflection of their middle-class backgrounds, availability of activities in the suburb (again related to class), and also their younger age.

Most of the girls seemed to have no clear plans about future jobs or careers, and none of the older group at Southlands appeared to be planning to take any higher education courses.

The firmest plans came from two friends in one friendship group (Southlands) who were planning to go into nursing. Others mentioned working in the travel and tourism industry, or becoming a commercial artist or a florist. When asked what they expected to be doing in ten years time, they acknowledged that they were likely to be married with a family, but all but one said that getting a career sorted out first was a priority. Some responses, showing this distinctly pragmatic tendency, were:

I'll probably be married—probably have kids—but I want my career sorted out first.

Somewhere I'd like to have a family—I'd like kids but it's not a major consideration—I don't know if I could handle the pressure—when I see what my Mum goes through.

Hopefully get a career is the first thing—have a family later on—*a lot* further on.

I wouldn't actually like to be married. I'd like a good steady job. I'd like to have kids but not be married.

Working—travelling around—I'm not having kids.

In reflecting an awareness of their likely futures both in the workforce and as mothers, these responses are consistent with recent Australian studies which have focussed on working-class teenage girls as discussed in chapter 1 (for example, Taylor, 1986; Wilson and Wyn, 1987). The responses illustrate the paid work/domesticity conflict experienced by teenage girls which we have also discussed. They also illustrate the complexities involved in the construction of femininity: while at one level girls may appear to be preoccupied with romance and personal relationships, at another they are intellectually aware of trends in society and their likely futures.

Girls watch the soaps

All the girls interviewed enjoyed watching television and all named soap operas among their favourite programmes, the most popular being *Home and Away*, *Neighbours* and *Days of Our Lives* (in that order). Most also enjoyed 'family shows' and 'comedy shows', while two mentioned their dislike of news and current affairs programmes. In general they watched television for enjoyment and relaxation, with one girl commenting that it 'takes you away from everyday life'. One said that watching television was:

Something else to do. I don't really get really wrapped up in shows, but some of them you can really relate to.

When asked why they particularly liked to watch soap operas, some replies were:

They take you away from reality—they don't exactly—but they make it like everything's happy and perfect with the world.

You know it's not real, but it's fun watching. It gives you a break from life.

The characters are like real life.

I like the characters—they feel like friends.

One girl claimed:

I like *Home and Away* the best of all the programmes I watch because it is an easily related programme, and it deals with everyday problems like Ros getting pregnant.

Another said that she liked the same programme:

...because it has a lot of action, comedy and a little bit of romance. Also the people playing the parts are teenagers, and it shows life isn't meant to be easy, especially when you're a teenager.

In relation to their ability to 'relate' to the programmes, most of the girls felt that the characters and events in soap operas were reasonably like characters and events in 'real life', although most also felt that the programmes were 'exaggerated' (this word was used frequently). For example, it was mentioned that in many soap operas 'characters get up out of bed without a hair out of place', although *Home and Away* and *Neighbours* were felt to be more 'realistic' in this regard. The girls all expressed the contradiction between feeling the programmes to be 'realistic', while at the same time knowing that they are 'not real':

I think the characters are fairly believable...but I still feel they're not real. You know they're not real.

I can see the people as real people—they're slightly exaggerated...but I still think it's pretty realistic.

They're basic problems like real life, though they may be exaggerated to keep the audience entertained. But basically the problems are ones you would come across. Like *Neighbours* it's like real life but it's not really the same problems they have...they're sort of exaggerated—the way they bring things out.

It is at this level, with the reactions and feelings associated with relationships, that the girls seem to be involved with the texts:

> Sometimes, if you've got a problem and that problem's on TV sometimes it helps you to get over it. You can sit and watch them and how they deal with it, and you think about it and it helps you get over yours... You don't exactly learn from it, but it helps you to think about it.

> It helps you make decisions.

The view that soap operas can sometimes help with personal problems was expressed by several of the girls, and another commented that the reactions of people were 'pretty normal' and 'close to home'. She continued:

> You feel it's actually happening to you. You know what you'd do if you were in that position.

Another replied:

> They sort of tackle everyday situations and you can see how it affects the other members of the family.

Some of the girls felt that they could also learn about social issues like drugs and AIDS from watching soap operas like *A Country Practice*. One girl (Southlands), when asked about her favourite programme, talked about it in class terms. She described the class conflict which emerged between two of the main characters in *Home and Away*, and continued:

> Bobby—the lower class girl—she doesn't get on with society—just about everybody's against her and there's quite a lot of friction built up there.

Although the girls said that they sometimes 'feel for' the characters, there was no evidence that the girls were identifying with particular characters, and only two said that they had a favourite character. Furthermore, where a favourite character was named, there was no indication that the character might be acting as a role model for the viewer, although one girl referred to the problems experienced when a favourite character left a programme:

> When Molly died on *A Country Practice* I finished with soapies altogether... I think I got turned off. I'd got attached to her—and I thought it's probably going to happen in other programs too—so I didn't watch soapies for a while.

In general, however, there was evidence that allegiances to characters did change, probably due to the multiple plots of the soaps, and to the focus on a number of main characters. In fact the allegiances of the girls seemed to lie with the programme as a whole rather than with individual characters. Significantly, when the girls mentioned particular soap opera characters, the discussion always focussed on their personalities rather than on appearance or looks.

Of the twelve girls at Southlands six were fans of *Days of Our Lives* and six disliked the programme, while at Hillview five out of the eight were fans. All the girls readily distinguished between *Days of Our Lives* and the evening soap operas which they watched. They saw *Home and Away* and *Neighbours* as being 'more realistic' and more relevant to them because they were Australian programmes and were about younger people. Despite this, the fans of *Days* had become involved with its characters and multiple stories. They had all originally become involved when the show was screened at 3.00 pm and they had been able to watch it when they got home from school. When the time was changed to 12.30 pm, some of the girls were then only able to watch in the holidays, but in four cases (all at Southlands) the show was taped by the girls' mothers, thus providing access to the day's episode when they got home from school. No girls from Hillview watched on a regular basis in this way.

As has been mentioned, *Days* was seen as less like real life than the prime-time soap operas, and it is significant that all the group shared this view regardless of whether or not they were fans. Some comments they made about *Days* were:

> It's more like the glamorous life—the clothes and things they wear just round the house—it's something you wouldn't really do.

> The characters and that—it's different from real life—exaggerated—I really enjoy it.

> I don't really think that's like real life at all—more something you'd wish for.

> They just go over the top. It's ridiculous.

Several made the point that the characters are in general older than them, and lead a wealthy lifestyle:

> It's about young couples relating to each other—their feelings and things that they do—their problems and marriage problems.

> They spend their lives going places—seeing things—at work and after work—meeting each other.

Despite the view that the people were 'rich', when asked what kinds of men and women were in the show, the girls said that they were 'ordinary' and 'just normal'. In relation to feelings and reactions of characters in the programme they once again saw them as 'fairly realistic with an exaggerated tone'. Some of the girls seemed to be more interested in the relationships and said that 'you could learn about relationships from watching *Days*.'

Others, when describing the programme, spoke first of the storyline rather than the characters and their relationships:

There's always something exciting happening.

It's mainly about drug busts, drug deals, murders, people fighting—and it carries on from episode to episode.

It's a bit far fetched—every episode is something to do with drugs/murders/rapes. Because it's so far fetched it makes it more interesting. . . . Sometimes when you watch it you think how you'd react in a situation.

However, other girls who were not fans said that it was 'too slow' and that they found it boring:

It's really slow—I like something happening—some action. Like in *The Bold and the Beautiful* they'll take a whole show to get engaged. It's boring—you've got to have a bit of action.

It turns you off a bit when it just drags on and you want something new to happen—*Days of Our Lives* keeps going and going.

When the girls were asked whether they thought that soap operas could be a bad influence upon adolescent girls, they were quite dismissive of the suggestion.

I wouldn't agree—they can't really do much harm—as long as you don't become really addicted — as long as you realise it's not actual reality.

Some people become addicted—I think they're afraid that we're going to become more involved with the show than with our own lives.

My mum doesn't worry about it—she realises I'm not going to be influenced by a TV show that's made up—they should realise that kids aren't going to be that stupid to be like that.

The fun and enjoyment the girls got from watching soap operas, as well as their emotional involvement in the pro-grammes, emerged as major themes in the discussions. The girls described the events and characters in the programmes as 'exaggerated' but were still able to relate to them and identify with the character's feelings and reactions. This also seemed to be the case with the daytime soap opera *Days*, even though the girls found this more removed from 'real life' experiences. There seems to be evidence of the double relationship of viewer with text identified by Ang (1985) in her research on watching *Dallas* and which Fiske describes as 'implication—extrication' (1987: p. 175). These girls are involved with the text emotionally, yet simultaneously distant from it. They are well aware that the stories are not like real life and yet are able to identify with the characters and their anxieties, in much the same way as some teenage girls may claim to read romances for relaxation and to escape daily problems, yet also claim to use them to learn how to behave on dates (Willinsky and Hunniford, 1986; Taylor, 1989a). Although the girls in this study seemed to be using soap operas to learn about relationships, the programmes did not seem to be acting as 'primers' for any of these girls. As has been mentioned, the girls did not seem to have favourite characters as role models, and their relationship with the programmes seemed complex and contradictory.

The context of viewing

Most soap opera viewing was done with other family members, particularly the girls' mothers, and it emerged that in most cases the viewing of *Days* began because the mothers were fans. One girl, explaining why she liked the programmes, said:

> I don't know—I'm addicted to *Days of Our Lives*—I can't miss an episode. I used to come home from school and Mum would be watching and you'd sit down and watch the show, and then I got interested and then they changed the time. We complained—we wrote to the *TV Weekly*. It didn't work though!

In the cases of the Southland students where the girls' mothers taped the programme for them on a regular basis, the girls watched as soon as they got in from school—often with their mothers. One girl said that she watched *The Young and the Restless* with her mother and then *Days* on the tape. One girl, who had said that she was particularly involved with the relationships in the programme, was selective in the way she viewed the tape:

> The ones I don't like—I just fast forward it—it doesn't matter because you've got so many different stories—you just fast forward until you get to a good conversation part.

Several of the girls said that they didn't like watching with other members of their families because of their tendency to 'make comments' all the time. It appeared that fathers and brothers were the main offenders with respect to soap operas:

> My Dad says, 'What's this stupid programme?' and then sits and watches it.

> My Dad's just the same—thinks most of the shows we watch are really silly—and then he sits down and watches them!

One had a twenty-year-old brother who used to get their mother to tape *Days* every day for him. Another commented:

> Most guys say, 'I wouldn't watch that sissy show'. And then you find out they do!

Most of the girls did their homework while watching television but they always stopped to watch their favourite programmes:

> Everything stops at 6.30 to watch *Home and Away*. If I've got homework to do in any other programme I won't stop.

In general it seemed to be common for the girls to watch television and do their homework in the advertisements, although one girl said:

> I often do my homework listening—looking up from time to time.

However, one mentioned that she didn't always get her homework done. One difference which emerged between the girls from the two schools was that at Hillview four of the girls were not allowed to watch television and do their homework at the same time, whereas none of the Southland girls experienced such parental control.

Talk about their favourite programmes featured prominently among the school friendship groups, and one girl became a *Days* fan when she first watched it at a friend's house. At the time when the interviews were carried out, the television programme *The Comedy Company* was very popular and apparently all the girls were 'going around talking like Kylie Mole'. (A nice irony here given that the character was apparently developed by listening to fourteen-year-old girls talking.) While there were differences in likes and dislikes within the friendship groups, viewing preferences did not seem to be a factor in the shaping of the groups.

The viewing patterns which emerged in this study indicate that some of the girls already show distinctly feminine relationships to television in terms of their preferences and viewing style. For example, in his research on family viewing practices, David Morley (1986) found that women preferred to watch fictional programmes such as soap operas in preference to other genres, as did the girls in this study. Morley also found that women were most likely to watch television while doing something else, such as ironing, and that they tended to feel guilty if they did otherwise. In contrast, men tended to give the television their undivided attention—without feeling guilty. Clearly, this difference reflects the fact that women continue to have prime responsibility for domestic work and, while in the home, continue to find tasks to do. Thus, in doing their homework while watching television the Southlands girls are already adopting a typically feminine style of viewing in the sense that they do not give the television their undivided attention. However, class factors may be important here, as well as gender, in shaping this style of viewing.

The study also showed that in their friendship groups at school the girls talked about the soap operas they watched with each other—illustrating the way in which representational cultural texts and lived social relations are interrelated. Such talk ('gossip') has been identified as an important aspect of women's culture in which soap operas have been identified as playing a central role (Brown, 1987). The girls in the study also seem to have been drawn into this women's culture through their mothers' soap opera watching practices, which included the use of video recordings to ensure that favourite soap operas could be watched. It seems that the home video recorder has enabled families to exert a good deal of control over their television viewing, although the study suggested that there were conflicts within their families over both television viewing and video recording.

Before attempting to draw conclusions from the case study, we will briefly discuss some of the characteristics of *Home and Away*, which emerged in the discussions as the favourite programme of most of the girls interviewed. We are particularly interested in highlighting the versions of femininity it offers.

'Home and Away'

Home and Away is an Australian prime-time soap opera produced by Channel 7, screened at 6.30–7.00 pm on each weeknight. The soap was first screened in 1988, and centres on Summer Bay, a small coastal town in New South Wales. Many of the main characters are young people in their late teens and consequently the programme is popular with young audiences. As we have seen, this was the most popular programme with the teenage girls interviewed in our case study. The coastal setting provides plot lines which centre on the beach, the surf life-saving club and the caravan park, and which allow for the introduction from time to time of characters who are on holiday or 'passing through'. Other locations are the store and the high school and the homes of the main characters. The introductory sequences to the programme, during which the characters are introduced, feature the surf and the beach prominently, though until fairly recently most of the action was filmed indoors.

This soap provides an interesting twist to the emphasis on family and kinship usually found in soap operas by focussing on foster parents Tom and Pippa Fletcher and their fostered children. Tom and Pippa are foster parents to a series of young people, and issues concerning 'real' parentage provides a continuing basis for plot material, particularly in the case of their foster daughter Bobby. Related, the ideal of the 'happy family' appears as a theme in the form of the desire to have a 'real' home and family and this notion is captured in the title itself and in the introductory theme song: 'Home and Away—with you every day'. The focus in *Home and Away* is on family relations and on relationships between the young people themselves—some of the latter being romantic relationships. Because of the fostering theme there is an emphasis on the relationships in the blended families. At the time of the interviews in 1988 a central storyline was concerned with one girl's pregnancy while still at school and her decision about whether she would keep the baby. Another storyline dealt with child abuse—in episodes in early 1990 Bobby reveals that she was beaten by her drunken stepfather when it becomes apparent that the same man is beating his daughter Sophie. The fact that the abuse comes from a *stepfather* in the case of Bobby and a *single father* in the case of Sophie leaves the ideal of a happy 'real family' intact.

In terms of versions of femininity offered by *Home and Away*, a number of the characters are strong and independent women. Bobby is something of a 'tomboy', dressing in jeans and without makeup, who is portrayed as someone who 'speaks her mind'. Other characters, for example Roo and Carly, are more traditionally feminine in both looks and behaviour. However, it is important to recall that one of the

Southlands girls seemed to view Bobby in terms of class rather than gender issues: 'Bobby—the lower class girl—she doesn't get on with society—just about everybody's against her and there's quite a lot of friction built up there. The relationships between the young women characters in *Home and Away* do not in general emphasise friendship and solidarity. As is typical with the soap genre, disputes and fights over boyfriends are commonplace, and Bobby has her share of disagreements.

It has been mentioned that the girls who were interviewed read the characters as 'ordinary' and did not comment on their appearance and looks. While the central characters of *Home and Away* are not outstandingly beautiful or striking, they are not unattractive either. Furthermore, some stereotyping does occur, though in a far from straightforward way. For example, a series of episodes screened in early 1990 centred on the problems that a new character, Greta, had in finding a boyfriend. Greta is tall and big built, with dark hair and glasses, and acutely concerned that, because of her looks, men aren't interested in her. She drinks beer and beats Martin at pool and thinks she is seen as 'one of the boys'. Her friend Marilyn, on the other hand, is slim, petite, sexy and blonde. In fact the notion that 'men prefer blondes' is undermined as Greta proves to be a more interesting person to the opposite sex. The storyline ends with Greta leaving Summer Bay with renewed confidence to 'do things' with her life, frightened off by Martin who falls in love with her and wants to settle down! Thus though there is an attempt to demolish a stereotype in these episodes through the *storyline*, it is done *through* the blatant stereotyping in terms of appearance and behaviour of the two female characters concerned. This stereotyping was such that it would have been most unlikely that any teenage girls would identify with Greta and aspire to be like her. Furthermore, the sequence is really another version of 'how to catch a man' and in no way challenges patriarchal gender relations despite the fact that Greta chooses to move on alone. So while programmers may be intentionally trying to overturn stereotypes (see Tulloch (1989) in relation to *A Country Practice*), the extent to which this can be done is questionable, given that oppositional ideologies are always presented within a range of dominant ideologies with which they conflict, as in the above example.

This is particularly evident when we consider the advertisements which are screened along with a particular programme, an important factor in considering the way in which a programme is viewed. It has been argued that advertisements may provide links with television programmes as well as contradictions: in other words there is nexus of 'interruption and flow', of 'continuity and conflict' between soaps and commercials (Tulloch, 1989). We have suggested that *Home and Away* is contradictory in terms of offering a range of images of femininity, and this is also the case with the advertisements.

The advertisements which are screened with *Home and Away* provide a collage of different characteristics of femininity which together construct a 'model woman' (Tulloch 1989: p. 126), and this ideal woman is constructed within patriarchal gender relations. The advertisements fall into three main categories: the first are those targetting a general teenage audience, for example Coca-Cola advertisements, which show attractive young people surfing and generally having fun, and also for fast-food outlets such as Pizza Hut, Big Rooster and Kentucky Fried Chicken; the second group are advertisements for skincare products, soap and perfume, which target young women and which present extremely stereotyped versions of femininity; and the third group are for food products, for example breakfast cereals, margarine and Quik chocolate milk, which mainly feature mothers with children. The versions of femininity offered emphasise looks and appearance, and women's domestic roles. During the episodes when the Greta story described above was screened, an advertisement for Impulse perfume spray was shown. In classic romantic style, the sequence shows a beautiful woman being pursued by a handsome stranger who gives her flowers. The accompanying slogan reads, 'Men can't help acting on Impulse'. In general, then, the advertisements screened with *Home and Away* offer traditional versions of femininity, and the Impulse sequence provides a particularly striking example. This makes it even more likely that the 'oppositional' aspects of the Greta story are likely to be lost among the blatant stereotyping of the two female characters which we have discussed.

Soap operas and femininity

> Like sands through the hourglass, so are the days of our lives.

This epigraph and the accompanying visual in the introduction to *Days* is illustrative of much about the soap opera genre. As we argued earlier, soap opera texts are open ended, ongoing and have a perpetual sense of irresolution. They parallel 'real'

time and explicitly make links with generalised everyday life
and experiences, and their titles often typify these features—
Days of Our Lives, Neighbours, EastEnders.

For the working-class and middle-class girls in this case
study, television viewing was an important spare-time activity,
and soap opera viewing occupied a significant place in their
everyday lives. The focus in this chapter has been on the ways
that this soap opera viewing, as an aspect of popular culture,
connects with the experiences of the teenage girls. In other
words, we are attempting to explore the interrelation between
soaps as representational cultural texts and the lived social
relations of the girls' sub-cultures. As Angela McRobbie (1984)
has argued in relation to the role of fantasy in popular fiction,
popular cultural texts are just as 'lived' as 'lived experience',
and often constitute the private moments of everyday experience. Similarly, Walkerdine (1986) argues for the disruption of
the common sense split between 'fantasy' and 'reality', and in
her study of a family watching a video of *Rocky II*, explores
'how people make sense of what they watch and how this
sense is incorporated into an existing fantasy structure' (1986:
p. 192). Popular cultural texts such as soap operas also inter-
sect with lived social relations in other more obvious ways. As
we have seen, soap opera characters and events are topics of
conversation in the day-to-day lives of fans.

In relation to soap opera viewing, it seems that the girls' real
life and fantasy worlds merge and allow them to rehearse
conflicts and problems which they experience in their lives.
As has been mentioned, this is not dissimilar to the way in
which teen romances seem to be used by some teenage girls.
However, although there are some similarities with romance
reading, television is in other ways a very different popular
cultural form. As we have discussed previously, television
narratives are more open to negotiation due to their polysemic
nature, and this is particularly the case with feminine genres
such as soap operas. The soaps offer a plurality of meanings
and articulations with other cultural texts, which results in
different readings, dependent upon the social situation of the
viewers.

Class and gender together structure cultural perspectives,
but in this study there were very few differences in the responses of the working-class and middle-class girls. In terms
of their views about soap operas, gender seemed to be a
unifying factor, with some class differences emerging in
relation to the context of viewing and in certain aspects of

spare-time activities. For example, several of the working-class girls watched videotapes of *Days of Our Lives* on a regular basis when they came home from school, and they also did their homework while watching television. However, the middle-class girls' spare time and television watching was subjected to more control by their parents.

In relation to the appeal and place of soap opera viewing in the lives of these teenage girls, there were many similarities with findings from studies of adult soap opera viewing. In their preferences and viewing patterns the girls were already showing well established feminine patterns in the use of television in their lives, and some seemed to be becoming initiated into the 'ritual pleasures' which are part of a culture of femininity. At this stage this culture was to some extent collective, with girls often watching the soaps with their mothers or with their friends, and also talking about the soaps at school—although for many adult women soap opera viewing may become a solitary and guilty pleasure (Morley, 1986).

In relation to the actual meanings made of the soap opera text, feminine genres like soap operas are typically open enough to allow for a variety of oppositional readings. The serial form and multiple characters and plots are characteristics which make this possible, as are other soap opera conventions like an 'emphasis on dialogue, problem solving and intimate conversation'; the portrayal of many of the male characters as sensitive men; and the construction of female characters who are often 'professional or otherwise powerful in the world outside the home' (Brown, 1987: p. 4). It is difficult to ascertain precisely what readings were being made at an ideological level by the girls in this study—a different kind of research focus would be needed. However, it is possible to make some tentative suggestions on the basis of the interviews and our discussion of *Home and Away*.

Certainly the whole focus on feelings and relationships in soap operas helps to legitimate and maintain girls' interests in these aspects of feminine culture, and particularly their preoccupation with romance. However, as we have shown, interest in the *romantic* aspects of the relationships did not emerge particularly strongly in the girls' discussions, nor are they given particular emphasis in their favourite soap, *Home and Away*. Previous research on romance reading indicated that girls would like more books which centre on other relationships—within the family and with friends (Taylor, 1989a). Perhaps this is part of the appeal of soap operas for this group? Family relationships and problems are usually central in soap operas, and the girls referred to them frequently in the interviews. This may be partially related to the contradictory social position between childhood and adult status which they occupy within their own families. In other words, age relations may be helping to structure their perspectives.

In chapter 1 we argued that gender identity for young women is centred on appearance and sexuality and that media texts are central in the construction of this identity. Although soap operas are targeted towards women as consumers, in fact there is less emphasis on appearance and looks than in many other media representations of femininity. Brown has noted in relation to soap opera that: '...this discourse of sexual power is not constructed around the male gaze. In the daytime soaps closeups of faces predominate almost to the exclusion of body shots. Facial closeups always include the whole face rather than segments of it. There are no unmotivated fragmented body shots. Thus the image of the body of women as sexual currency is absent...' (1987: p. 19).

In contrast to this kind of representation, Brown argues that the power of the female body to create (that is biologically, through pregnancy) is central in soap operas, along with the social rules which operate to contain that power. Here she is referring to the prevalence of themes concerned with paternity, maternity and kinship. For example, as we noted in the previous section, the focus on fostering in *Home and Away* offers scope for exploring these themes. While soap operas may use patriarchal myths, they are structured and played with in such a way as to allow them to be questioned by their audiences. For example, the 'equilibrium of a happy, stable family is constantly there in the background, but is never achieved' (Fiske, 1987: p. 180). Thus, as well as legitimating and affirming feminine values, soap opera texts can also be seen at another level as challenging dominant patriarchal ideologies, and providing an alternative to the pervasive images of woman-as-sex-object which were discussed earlier.

One further significant aspect of the role of soap operas as cultural texts relates to the pleasure and enjoyment which the girls derived from watching soap operas. Feminist work on the education of girls has focussed on gender ideologies and discourses relating to femininity, and has taken little account of fantasy. Research with adult soap opera viewers shows that it is possible for viewers to 'bracket' reality for a while and be involved at an emotional level with the programme—as a kind of 'time out' from the 'real world'. Ang (1985) argues that this does not preclude a feminist consciousness and, as we have seen, there was evidence in the case of these girls of the double relationship of viewer with text. As has been found in studies of adult soap opera viewers, the girls were able to be simultaneously involved with the programmes emotionally and yet also critical and distant. As we have noted, Ang (1985) has suggested that viewers may experience pleasure from the fantasy world of soap operas at a quite different level from the ideological content of the programmes. In her view:

> Fantasy is therefore a fictional area which is relatively cut off and independent. It does not function in place of, but beside, other dimensions of life. . . It is a dimension of subjectivity which is a source of pleasure *because* it puts 'reality' in parentheses, because it constructs imaginary solutions for real contradictions which in their fictional simplicity and their simple fictionality step outside the tedious complexity of the existing social relations of dominance and subordination. (1985: p. 135)

Are we to conclude, then, that the ideological content of soap operas is irrelevant, given that the programmes appear to be a source of pleasure at the level of fantasy and given that their open form allows oppositional readings to be made? While on the one hand it is clear that viewers do not necessarily uncritically take on board the discourses in soap operas, such popular cultural texts, along with 'real-life' experiences, nevertheless become part of a repertoire of ways of thinking about and talking about 'being female'. Consequently, it is this *range of available discourses* which is drawn on in the construction of femininity and which is crucial in providing the framework within which this takes place. The discourses of soap operas *may* be relatively progressive in that they play with the myths of patriarchy. But that does not mean that alternative discourses, extending patriarchal versions of femininity, could not be more empowering—particularly for teenage girls and young women.

It also needs to be stressed that structural conditions will set limits on the resistance which can occur, and its political effectiveness. In chapter 1 we discussed the conflicts which teenage girls express resulting from three sets of contradictory discourses about how they should behave. These contradictions centre on their futures (both in the paid workforce and as mothers), on sexuality, and on issues relating to age and maturity. We argued that these conflicts work together to define femininity predominantly in the private domestic sphere and, with romance as a central theme, towards marriage and motherhood.

Soap operas may help girls explore independent futures through some of the strong women characters, but the ideal of 'the family' is always there as well—even if it is rarely achieved. Furthermore, while marriages and romances never last, one of the conventions of the genre is that central characters must be 'available' for 'lasting' romantic love (Lovell, 1981: p. 50). The potential for such oppositional or resistive readings is important, though it is probable that teenage girls' limited life experiences would make them less likely to make oppositional readings than older women viewers. In the light of the conflicts which teenage girls express about their futures it would seem unlikely that the contradictions offered by soaps will be very helpful to them. If we also consider the overall 'flow' of the programmes, where, as we have noted, the advertisements screened along with soap operas tend to focus on appearance and looks and present more traditional versions of femininity, we can only conclude that the images of femininity are fairly narrow and limited and do little to challenge the patriarchal gender order. In a situation where traditional versions of femininity are maintained by a majority of representational cultural texts, we cannot feel optimistic about the repertoire which soaps offer to teenage girls, and agree with Lovell's assertion:

> . . . whether we are concerned with ideology, or with structures of feeling and sensibility, it is necessary to avoid the temptation of mistaking what is *actually* achieved by particular production teams, and the limits within which they work in these respects, with what it is *possible* to do within any particular type of programme. Because the dominant structures of feeling and sensibility are reproduced in the programme, it does not follow that different structures of feeling and sensibility might not have been made much more prominent, *despite* the various constraints under which the programme makers worked. (1981: p. 48)

4

Romancing the girl: fiction, fantasy and femininity

Teacher/librarians are duty bound to present balance in the world views to which students are exposed. We must not present them with an unreal, romanticised world where women completely abdicate responsibility for themselves, where 'love' is accompanied either by ringing bells or male aggression, where the sexual attraction between male and female is the only thing which matters. Such a world does not exist. (Altus, 1984b: p. 129)

I observe in these (romance) books neither an effective top-down propaganda effort against women's liberation, nor a covert flowering of female sexuality. Instead, I see them as accurate descriptions of certain selected elements of female consciousness...The books...define a set of relations, feelings, and assumptions that do indeed permeate our minds. They are mass paperbacks not only because they are easy to read pablum but also because they reflect...commonly experienced psychological and social elements in the daily lives of women. (Snitow, 1984: pp. 259–60)

The place that romance fiction plays in girls' lives, and might play in classroom reading selection, remains a vexatious issue for researchers and educators. The issue is seen to typify many of the complexities associated with the status and nature of popular cultural texts: the power and ownership of patriarchal consumerism; the value placed on women's interests and women's experiences; the ideological and commercial fashioning of femininity for girls and young women; the nature of reading and fiction in people's lives; and the school authorisation of suitable classroom curriculum materials.

Romance fiction is clearly a highly successful commercial

enterprise which draws its support from many different age groups of girls and women. Adult romance novels not only attract an American audience of more than 20 million women, but one out of four adult women in North America reads romance fiction at an average rate of four or more per month, and paperback romances are translated and sold by the millions in at least twenty other countries around the world (Thurston, 1987: p. vii). Although the average print run for an adult romance is 150 000 copies, print runs for some romance lines are known to be as high as 500 000. Compare this with an average run of 10 000 for an Australian novel.

Teen romance fiction is similarly popular, given the smaller commercial market from which it draws. On the American market the genre accounted for 35 per cent of non-adult paperbacks sold by the B. Dalton bookseller chain (Lam, 1986: p. 17), making teen romance fiction one of the top three kinds of books read and purchased by girls (Christian-Smith, 1987: p. 368). And in Australia Maylyn Lam cites comments by the Australian national sales manager of Scholastic that even successful Australian writers like Joan Phipson and Colin Thiele can be outsold by a ratio of 3:1 with a 'good romance title' for adolescents (Lam, 1986: p. 18). The publicity and marketing manager of Bantam's distribution agency in Australia similarly claimed that teen romances are the company's strongest Australian seller (Lam, 1986: p. 18).

Unquestionably romance series novels sell quickly and widely, and the romance fiction business is *big* business, even with teenagers. In 1979 Scholastic Book Service launched its young adult romance series—*Wildfire*—and the first teen romance books hit the market. The *Wildfire* series sold over 2.25 million copies in the first two years and made a path for the proliferation of other young adult romance series. *Sweet Valley High* (Bantam) and *Sweet Dreams* (Bantam)—both packaged as 'the designer jeans of the book market' (Willinsky and Hunniford, 1986: p. 18)—are two of the American series to be commercially successful in Australia. The books are presented as a numbered series and come complete with matching logos and similar cover designs; they are thus eminently 'collectible' and 'swappable'.

The American series, until recently, dominated the field for Australian girls, but in 1988 Australian Consolidated Press released a new Australian series called *Dolly Fiction*, marketed as an extension of *Dolly* magazine. *Dolly Fiction* follows the packaging patterns of the earlier young adult romance series:

the books clearly belong to a series (as is evident from the similarity of their covers, titles, and general layout) and they are numbered for easy collection and consumption. The major difference with this series is that it obviously hopes to trade off the success of *Dolly* magazine—a magazine with a circulation of almost 250 000 per month. *Dolly Fiction* claims to offer girls more of what they 'loved' in the magazine. 'You just can't get enough!' is the advertising slogan.

The popularity of romance fiction

The commercial sales figures indicate quite clearly how successful the marketing ventures of the romance publishing houses have been, but the prior question is why has this been possible: why do so many young women find romance series fiction desirable. At one level, romance reviewers like Rosemary Guiley (1983) see that the enduring appeal of romance fiction for teens is quite natural: simply a result of the 'inevitability' of teenage girls' preoccupation with boys: 'As long as teenage girls are interested in the opposite sex, young adult romances are sure to have a place on the bookshelf' (Guiley, 1983: p. 95).

But teenage girls are obviously interested in many things other than 'the opposite sex', and there would seem to be a broad range of material for girls to read. Young adult publishing, for instance, has become an important commercial venture of the last twenty years, but it hasn't posed any threat to romance formula novels: many girls seem to prefer romance novels. Bea Knodel (1982) asks:

> ...why, when quality young adult books are steadily improving, when serious authors who are skilled writers are publishing books with reasonably rounded characters, carefully constructed plots, and themes of genuine concern to adolescents, young women readers in droves are choosing instead books in which the writing is pedestrian at best, the characters range from plastic to cardboard, the plots are absolutely predictable, and the themes are almost exclusively 'boy gets girl', or rather 'girl gets boy'? (Knodel, 1982: p. 1)

Knodel attempts to account for these preferences of young women by suggesting that there are three possible ways in which young adult fiction has largely failed them. Publishing houses—she argues—still predominantly produce material which concentrates on masculine worlds and interests, which presents female characters who would rather watch than act, and which portrays female protagonists who 'do not show characteristics most intelligent young women would wish to emulate' (Knodel, 1982: p. 4). As we argued in chapter 1, the dominant discourse of adolescence—and one reflected rather obviously in much young adult fiction—is a strongly masculinist discourse (Hudson, 1984). The identity crises and social alienation that young women must deal with, as they struggle over the taking up of various gendered subject positions, is seldom addressed in young adult fiction. Instead the female characters constructed in adolescent literature are often, as Knodel demonstrates, victims: of rape, of drugs, of unwanted pregnancies, of crime. Their characters are 'read' in terms of their relationships with more powerful groups like their families, their boyfriends, their employers.

In addition, young women are consistently positioned to receive a steady flow of images which exhort them to be interested in romance, in boys, and in the preparation of the body for both romance and boys. From these positions, becoming 'feminine' is seen to be closely related to becoming 'romantic' (and therefore heterosexual) and inscribing the body appropriately. The desire to be feminine, and therefore attractive to men, becomes intimately connected with the dominant features of romance ideology. It thus becomes important for girls to 'know' about romance, to know how to prepare for successful heterosexual relationships. In this way, romance fiction works beside other cultural practices in the construction of female desire.

The 'fantasy' in romance fiction connects with aspects of female desire to offer girls an escape from the apparent contradictions of growing up female. As Walkerdine suggests, popular cultural texts directed at young women position them to look for a 'prince' (1984), to look for an escape route from the tensions and contradictions of lived gender relations in a patriarchal society. The 'fantasy' does this by positioning girls discursively, so that they are prepared to accept romance as a solution to the contradiction. In this way, girls are prepared for entry into heterosexual practices—for romantic love in particular—by being presented with and inserted into ideological and discursive positions which serve to produce and reproduce femininity. But this 'insertion' is not necessarily passive, it is struggled over, and girls adopt only a shaky and partial version of femininity as a result of the struggle. Becoming feminine, then, continues to be a struggle. It represents the attempt to reconcile the irreconcilable; to seek coherence where there clearly is none; to find solutions to an endless stream of 'problems'.

Romance fiction can, in one way, be read as a solution to the particular 'problem' of becoming feminine. It offers the fantasy of a caring, loving and sensitive male who will eventually be won, if a woman can demonstrate such qualities as physical attractiveness, moral virtuousness, and a willingness to be submissive. There then becomes a reason for the fetish with the body, the face, the hair and the clothes; a reason for self-sacrificing one's own interests and needs; a reason for quelling anger and indignation at the humiliating subject positions on offer. 'Some day my prince will come'—a girl must be ready. Love makes the pain and anxiety of becoming feminine tolerable, for it offers the promise of an idyllic resolution to the seemingly intolerable set of contradictions that becoming feminine represents.

Seen from a different perspective, the popularity of romance fiction can perhaps also be read as a reflection of the failure of patriarchal marriage to address women's basic emotional needs, as an unvoiced protest against patriarchal arrangements. For instance, Janice Radway (1984) argues that romance reading is fuelled by dissatisfaction and disaffection, that women read romance as a temporary 'declaration of independence' from the social roles of wife and mother. In the romance, women are likely to find a fantasy which resolves the anxieties and tensions of reality; a fantasy in which love and romance are possible; a fantasy in which Mr Right will come along. And it is the fantasy which gives some 'pleasure' to women as they live out the reality of patriarchal social relationships. As Ien Ang warns: 'The practice of consuming popular fiction may not be directly conducive to political radicalism...but as part of female existence within the status quo it helps to make women's lives more cheerful, just as, for instance, music, dance or gossip do' (1987: p. 657).

Ang argues that the *fictionality* of romance fiction puts reality in brackets, it creates a space for its consumers to be 'out of the complexities of real life for a while'. This unreality is also addressed by Tania Modleski (1982) in her work with soap operas and romance texts. Modleski similarly notes the danger of underestimating the role romance fiction plays in many women's lives, and of the tendency for feminist critics to want to dissociate themselves intellectually from the seductiveness of such texts. She argues that even though mass-produced fantasies may be at 'the service of patriarchy' (p. 104), they obviously give women pleasure. Perhaps, Modleski argues, the reading of romance fiction would be better considered as part of 'the varied and complex strategies women use to adapt to circumscribed lives and to convince themselves that limitations are really opportunities' (Modleski, 1982: p. 38).

Modleski uses the term 'adaptation'—adaptation by women to unsatisfactory and circumscribed lives—and this is similar to Walkerdine's (1986) consideration of the concept of fantasy in popular cultural texts. Watching a Hollywood movie is not, Walkerdine claims, simply an escape from drudgery into dreaming: 'it is a place of desperate dreaming, of hope for transformation' (Walkerdine, 1986: p. 196). In her discussion of a family viewing of *Rocky II*, she observes that: 'Although it is easy to dismiss such films as macho, stupid and fascist, it is more revealing to see them as fantasies of omnipotence, heroism and salvation. They can thus be understood as a counterpoint to the experience of oppression and power-lessness' (Walkerdine, 1986: p. 172).

This is largely possible with romance fiction because of the subject matter it draws upon. In chapter 3 we noted the strong emphasis in 'the soaps' towards the family and human relationships, and this is mirrored in many ways in romance fiction. Teen series, in particular, feature the crises and anguish of female friendship and family relationships, as sub-themes accompanying the rocky road to 'true (hetero-sexual) love'. In this way romance novels fashion a form of acceptable femininity whose touchstone is a particular style of heterosexual love.

Fashioning the feminine through romance fiction

Romance fiction largely operates in and around a construct of 'love', and it is a recognition of this which gives coherence to the fiction. Most of the actions in the novels are circumscribed by 'love', and it is this construct which makes the female characters' behaviour understandable and acceptable. The love of the adult romance novel is 'full of uncertainty, passion and pain when it seems unattainable; full of security and rosy warmth when permanently bestowed' (Altus, 1984a: p. 71).

Not surprisingly, teen romances—like their adult counter-parts—similarly position readers to accept that love is 'of itself a career' (Altus, 1984b: p. 128). The books usually focus upon the first meeting, the courting, and the final blissful culmination (in a kiss), of an adolescent girl's infatuation with a boy. The progress of the infatuation is the girl's dominant interest in life, often interfering with her school work, with her hobbies, with her family, with her friendships with other teenagers. All must be sacrificed if the path of the love affair is to run smoothly, and girls in teen romances will go to quite extraordinary lengths to achieve their goals.

The sexuality and passion of these romances comes in varying degrees of intimacy, and the teen romances, on the whole, are 'squeaky clean' in terms of direct reference to sexual behaviour. While they are still dominated by the quest for 'love', love in this case usually means a single, 'steady' relationship with one boy. 'Clean romance is the appeal of these novels', claims Guiley (1983: p. 93), 'there's no sex in these books—physical encounters are limited to a few kisses and embraces'.

But this is not the case in many of the more recent adult romances. Many of them contain explicit sexual scenes, and the sexual overtones are noticeable throughout the novels. Thurston (1987), for instance, notes that since 1972 the popular romance genre has been divided into two basic types—the sweet romance and the erotic romance—with the fundamental difference between them being 'the presence or absence of specific sexual behavioral norms and explicit sexual activities' (p. 7). However, while Thurston argues that these new erotic novels 'challenge the traditional power relationships between men and women' and depict 'a more balanced power alignment as natural and expected' (p. 8), a more commonly held view is that the erotic romances are more readily positioned with pornographic discourses.

In a discussion of the sexuality constructed in the world of Harlequin novels, Snitow (1984) claims that in these novels, as with pornography, 'the joys of passivity, of helpless abandon, of response without responsibility are all endlessly repeated, savored, minutely described' (pp. 268–9). Like other feminist researchers in this field (Altus, 1984a and 1984b; Walkerdine, 1984), Snitow notices how frequently romance fiction subjects women and girls to male cruelty and callousness. In these texts women will be bruised, broken and belted; they will be raped and humiliated; they will be imprisoned and rejected (see, for example, the extracts quoted by Altus, 1984a and 1984b). 'Cruelty, callousness, coldness, menace, are all equated with maleness and treated as a necessary part of the package', claims Snitow (1984). The romance formula offers expectation of male violence and the potential to tame aspects of this violence by passive acceptance and respect for male domination.

Some of the ways in which popular cultural texts prepare and position young women to accept this passivity and submissiveness can be traced through analyses of girls' comics—an initial preparation for adolescent and adult romance reading. Walkerdine (1984) notes how in English pre-teen comics like *Bunty* and *Tracy*, girls are produced as *victims*, and shown how to suffer in silence as a response to the cruelty or misfortune bestowed upon them.

> Girls are victims of cruelty but they rise above their circumstances by servicing and being sensitive to others—selflessness. The girl who services is like the beautiful girl whose rewards for her good deeds is to be taken out of her misery; she is freed by the prince. The semiotic chain slides into romance as the solution, with the prince as saviour. It is here that girls are produced as victims ready to be saved...(1984: p. 175)

Girls in these comics, and later in the teen romances, typically show no anger at this cruelty and injustice. Romantic heroines do not get angry: their victory is in their passivity and helpfulness, which contrasts with selfishness, anger, greed and jealousy. Anger therefore is wholly negative. One result of this passivity and selflessness is that while the good girl will act for others, she will not act for herself.

Angela McRobbie's work (1982) with the English teen comic *Jackie* indicates similar patterns and formulas. Romance in these comics is 'the language of passivity, *par excellence*' argues McRobbie (1982: p. 280).

> Girls can take humiliation and be all the more attractive for it, as long as they are pretty and unassertive. Boys can be footballers, pop stars, even juvenile delinquents, but girls can only be feminine. The girl's life is defined through emotions—jealousy, possessiveness and devotion. Pervading the stories is an elemental fear, fear of losing your boy, or of never getting one. Romance as a code or a way of life, precipitates individual neurosis and prohibits collective action as a means of dealing with it. (1982: p. 281)

The private world of the emotions is the world for the romance heroine. She is alone: emotionally isolated except for the possible ministrations of a female friend who may or may not be totally trustworthy. All women are potential enemies because all are looking for men. Consequently the quest for love is a lone quest and it is in deadly earnest, because the promise of a loving and lasting heterosexual relationship is seen to demonstrate the successful acquisition of femininity.

Not surprisingly, the characters developed in these single quest novels are notoriously stereotyped, and this is typically in keeping with the pornographic character of the fiction. Such characters need no past and no context, considerations that are relatively unimportant in the dominant movement of the formula. The romantic heroine is a stereotype, in love with love. She is also inscribed by romance, and is preoccupied with her clothing, with her hair, with the shape of her body. She is also, as Snitow (1984) argues, always in a state of emotional arousal, ready for the arrival of 'the phallus', but yet constantly alert to the need to hide her desires, to protect her reputation, to cover up all signs of sexual feeling. She is also always attractive, although she may not initially think so and needs external verification of her feminine/romantic appearance. Usually she belongs to no ethnic group or religion, and exists in a buffered unreal social group where money and privilege are seldom discussed. Family circumstances are usually not described, nor are social values.

Heroes are similarly stereotypical. Like the heroine, they are occasionally metamorphosed during the course of the fiction so that their full sensual attractiveness is revealed, but unlike the heroine, they are never really known and understood. Their actions are often bewildering to the heroine. Snitow (1984) suggests that in the adult Harlequin romance world all tensions and problems arise from the fact that male and female are incapable of communicating with each other. The sexes, she suggests, 'find each other utterly mystifying' (Snitow, 1984: p. 260). The romance formula is then about bridging this gulf in such a way that the essential hardness and superiority of the male are not totally destroyed. He must become softer, but not 'too soft' if he is to be of service to the woman (Snitow, 1984: p. 273).

Other characters are always secondary to the romance, and are often lampooned if they do not fit the parameters of the romance ideology. 'Slags' and 'drags'—as we saw in chapter 1—are the points of polarity. Ugly, mannish or assertive women are ridiculed as being unfeminine, as are bitchy women who don't know how to treat their men, and flirts or sexually permissive women who flaunt their desire. Teen romances also often feature parent figures in stereotypical caring roles, epitomising the fantasy of the loving marriage, the ultimate goal of the romance. Parents support the teenage girl's preoccupation with love, and mothers in particular worry for her if she has no boyfriend or no dates. Mothers also understand the pain of love, knowing that silent suffering in private is part of the 'game' of romance.

The romantic construction of femininity, then, seems to rely on a number of key themes, codes, or features, most of them connected to the heroine's quest for love—for domesticated sexuality—and the resultant qualities of femininity such a quest is seen to demand. There are two important issues to remember, however, in a consideration of such a construction of femininity. Popular cultural texts like the romance series novels are not static, they are both *mass* and *dynamic*. They are, as Thurston reminds us (1987), constantly reshaped in response to market forces and perceived reader demand, although the reshaping may not fundamentally alter the romance formula. As Linda Christian-Smith observed in her American study of teen romance novels from 1942 to 1982 (Christian-Smith, 1987), the codes constructing femininity (identified in this study as romance, beautification and sexuality) stayed remarkably stable during the 40 years covered. Changes were, Christian-Smith argued, 'not of a great magnitude'.

The way in which women and girls 'read' romance fiction is clearly also of significance. If the romance has done its job well—if the seams are hidden and the coherence is complete— it should construct an absorbing tension between sexual excitement, domestic security and romantic opportunity. The fact that many romance series have floundered, that some romance writers are infinitely more popular than others, and that romance publishing houses spend huge sums surveying their readers for evaluation of particular titles (Guiley, 1983; Thurston, 1987), is testimony to the fact that it is possible to get the formula 'right'. And if there is a formula, there is a reading practice, a way to read such texts so that they will be produced in desirable and attractive ways. Romance readers know the formula because they know the reading practice.

The third and fourth sections of this chapter will consider both of these perspectives. The dynamic nature of popular romance fiction will initially be addressed through an analysis of a modern and local teen romance series, *Dolly Fiction* (first published in 1988). In addition, girls' responses to this new series, and to the reading of other teen romance novels, will be the focus of the last section of the chapter.

The world of Dolly Fiction

As we have already seen, Carol Thurston (1987) suggests that the usual criticism made of contemporary romance fiction as 'the opiate of the female masses' is inaccurate and excessively generalised. Instead she argues that 'the most evolved erotic romances portray a feminine consciousness that has to do not only with sexual liberation but also with economic self-sufficiency' (p. 11).

While it is unwise to group the entire *Dolly Fiction* series together, or to regard the series as 'evolved erotic romances', it could be said—almost categorically—that the first eighteen teen romances released under this series in 1988–89 do not support Thurston's assertion about the positive influence for feminism of romance fiction. Rather than drawing upon feminist discourses, this series connects most obviously and most directly with the discourses of romance ideology explored earlier in this chapter. The series makes only minor token gestures to 'economic self-sufficiency', to the reality of women at work, or to women's changing place in society. Its major gesture, however, is directly towards the construction of a narrow and stereotypical version of romantic femininity.

The series has grown directly out of the success of *Dolly* magazine: an Australian magazine aimed very much at the eleven to fourteen age range, and holding down a key spot in the Australian magazine stakes for young women of this age. *Dolly Fiction* has obviously been designed as the Australian answer to the USA's *Sweet Dreams* and *Sweet Valley High*, and packaged similarly. It comes as a 'series'—each volume is numbered, and each cover has the same graphic format. As with the American books, the covers feature a photograph of a teen model, often models who appear regularly in *Dolly* magazine. The model has the same hair and eye colouring as the book's heroine, and a photograph of her is placed centre on a single colour cover. In keeping with the series nature of the books, the word 'DOLLY' is printed in large capitals across the top of the cover, whereas the title and author of the book are printed in much smaller type on the bottom. Twelve different writers' names feature on the covers, although some of these names may well be pseudonyms for the same person, as is typical with much series writing.

The titles for the books—when taken with the back and inside cover promotions—unambiguously position the reader for a formula romance:

1 THE LOOK OF LOVE by Margaret Pearce
2 BROKEN PROMISES by Katie Lee
3 GOOD TIMING by Trisha Trent
4 MY TYPE OF WRITER by Jaye Francis
5 WHO DO YOU LOVE? by Marianne Vaughan
6 I'VE GOT A SECRET by Mary Forrest
7 IN TOO DEEP by Linda Hollan
8 SHE'S A REBEL by Mary Forrest
9 STROKE OF LUCK by Alice Adams
10 SUMMER ESCAPE by Chris Kelson
11 FIRST IMPRESSIONS by Jaye Francis
12 SHE'S GOT THE BEAT by Gina Walsh
13 BOYS NEXT DOOR by Trisha Trent
14 YOU MUST REMEMBER THIS by Katie Lee
15 DESIGNS ON YOU by Jaye Francis
16 IS HE FOR REAL? by Suzanne Lennox
17 MY SISTER'S BOYFRIEND by Mary Forrest
18 HOLD ON TIGHT by Kerryn Ramsey

Interestingly, several of these title words can be recognised as puns once the back cover promotion has been read. *In Too Deep* has a windsurfing heroine, *Stroke of Luck* a swimming star, *Designs on You* a clothes designer, *My Type of Writer* an amateur journalist, and *Hold on Tight* a dog-walker. Despite this apparent playfulness, the titles, however, construct a typical concept of romance. *Dolly Fiction* titles suggest that romance is observable (*The Look of Love*), and typified by a number of specific features, some of which include: luck in the 'game' of love (*Good Timing, Stroke of Luck*); secrets and promises (*Broken Promises, I've Got a Secret, You Must Remember This*); female jealousy (*My Sister's Boyfriend, Hold on Tight*); emotional intensity (*In Too Deep*); and a girl's need to keep an ever vigilant eye for a likely romantic scenario (*Boys Next Door, Summer Escape*).

In the 1989 advice circular to likely writers for the *Dolly Fiction* series (Byrne, 1989), the series editor described the stories she wanted in this way:

The stories *are* romances, but we believe we can examine other issues within the genre and still have books which are a good read, while having something worthwhile to say as well. We're talking positive role models here!....Our books can be funny—some of the best ones are—and they don't have to end happily, or with a kiss etc, although some form of positive resolution from the heroine is always preferable...We want to show girls interested in and pursuing things other than boys—some of the time anyway.

The series editor's requests are not easily read from the first eighteen *Dolly* titles. The only 'other issues' to be discussed occur as very minor aspects of the texts. Teenage drinking gets a stereotypically superficial mention in numbers 1, 7 and 16; drug-taking is fairly unrealistically introduced in 17; female sexual assault is dealt with stereotypically in 10 and 14, when male intervention saves the day for the heroine; and male homosexuality and AIDS are rather ambiguously discussed in one chapter of number 6. On a more political front, urban redevelopment gets a minor hearing in 8, when a teenage boy organises his neighbourhood—including his girlfriend—to fight against the loss of an inner-city park area, and simplistic pleas for cultural tolerance are made in 8 and 9. The dominant story movement in all of the texts is, however, completely linked with the girl–boy relationship, with the 'romance'. It would seem that, despite the *aims* of this series, the generic conventions of the romance were too difficult to evade. It may well have been virtually impossible for writers of this series to construct the stories Belinda Byrne claims to want, within the possible—and recognisable, therefore commercially success-ful—generic conventions of the formula novel.

The 'romance' follows a very predictable pattern in the series. In fourteen of the eighteen titles, the story begins with a romantic/feminine novice, and the story turns on her metamorphosis—her fashioning—into a romantic/feminine convert. Even in the other four titles, the heroine is simply not yet the *complete* romantic, although she has a boyfriend, and knows something of 'love', she has still more to learn. The typical novice doesn't think she needs a boyfriend:

> . . . this year wasn't going to be easy. How was she going to juggle all the elements of her life, keep everyone happy, and pass her exams? At least, she thought thankfully, I haven't got a boyfriend to worry about. (no. 9: p. 2)

Or she doesn't attract boyfriends:

> I've been told I'm attractive and maybe it's true, I don't know, but it doesn't seem to help me find a boyfriend. (no. 7: p. 2)

She thinks she is 'different' from other girls:

> . . . she just didn't fit in here. She didn't look like the other girls at school. She didn't even own any make-up, let alone know how to use it . . . (no. 18: p. 13)

Why, oh why was she so plain, and stuck with elderly parents, and treated like an outsider at school? (no. 1: p. 5)

Fortunately not all parents are 'elderly' and unaware of the girl's needs. Most of the mothers in these novels are keen to see their daughters make the transition to romantic femininity:

Kyla giggled as she sat down at Emma's dressing table. 'Mum will be rapt,' she said happily. 'She's always reading fashion magazines and she loves to see me getting dressed up...' (no. 6: p. 42)

Mothers know what it's like:

There was a quiet knock on her door which she knew would be her mum's. She loved her mum more than anyone in the entire world, but right now she was the last person she wanted to see. Mothers knew too much. They had radar which alerted them to their children's suffering. (no. 14: p. 41)

They have 'knowing smiles' (no. 16: p. 114), 'mother's intuition' (no. 16: p. 140), and sound advice about the game of love:

'Darling, life's not like those romance novels you read, full of dramas and traumas and lashings of emotion... You did the right thing.'
'Mum!'... she was making it sound so sensible and mature and boring. I didn't feel... like the heroine in some stupid novel. I felt empty and sad and confused. 'You don't understand.'
'Don't I?' She gave me a quick kiss... (no. 16: p. 141)

The metamorphosis—the fashioning of the girl into the woman, of the pre-romantic child into the sexual female adolescent—hinges usually on one of three plot tensions. The novice may have to carve out her new romantic identity by inscribing her body romantically: she must be 'made-over' in the way that teen magazines make-over the ordinary girl into the desirable, 'feminine' girl. She may need a weight loss (1 and 3), and will almost certainly need different clothing and makeup (9 and 10). The most important problem the girls face when they finally get asked for a date is, 'What will I wear?'

'You won't believe what happened to me this afternoon,' she exclaimed when Rachel picked up the phone. 'What?' Rachel's voice had the same excited tone as Mandy's. 'Cameron asked me to go to the movies with him on Saturday night!' 'That's great!' **Then came the serious question.** 'What are you going to wear?' (no. 18: p. 35—emphasis added)

In this particular story, Mandy stereotypically persuades her father (not her mother) to give his little girl $100 to spend on clothes. Even though her mother later complains about this, and the amount is reduced to $50, Mandy already has $50 saved from her part-time work, so the grand total is still enough to do a reasonable 'make-over' job. When it is done—with the help of girlfriend Rachel (who knows all about what colours, styles and impressions will be 'right' for the shift from girl to sexual identity, and who is prepared to spend an entire Saturday 'doing' the makeup and hair job for her) the 'new' Mandy goes down to show her family. She wears a tight-fitting black dress, 'cut just above the knee', which 'accentuated every curve in her toned-up body'. Her hair was pulled back into an 'elegant French plait', and the new makeup gave her face 'a touch of glamour'. She is now, as her friend announces, no longer a child. She is 'the new Mandy Harrison!' (p. 47): the romantic/feminine young woman.

Once 'made-over'—or if the girl was already romantically inscribed—a second plot twist is possible. The girl may be fooled by falseness, either from other 'bitchy' girls (1, 3, 6, and 8), or from irresponsible, non-husband material boys (5, 7, 10, and 12). The 'true' romance event will, however, ensure her safe passage through these murky waters and guide her towards a greater understanding of the acceptable faces of femininity. Jealousy, overt sexuality, public gossiping, and vanity are outside the framework, as is association with boys who might jeopardise the girl's virginity and safety. The romantic girl—the feminine girl—is in search of the first awakening: the kiss. This marks her passage into womanhood. She must stay virginal until this passage is completed.

Helping people with problems becomes the third, and most popular plot twist. Girls are 'worriers' (17), who need to look after their little sisters (17), big sisters (13), girlfriends (11, 14), boyfriends (2, 4, 8), and even elderly neighbours' dogs (18). They are 'helpers' who unselfishly do what needs to be done for others to find happiness—usually romantic happiness. By helping others, they, too, are often rewarded by finding their own romance. Number 17 entirely revolves around an older sister's concern for her younger sister's reputation and safety once younger sister takes up with a drug-taker. Older sister, in this story, even goes out with her younger sister's ex-boyfriend, in an attempt to make her younger sister jealous of, and therefore happy to return to, the old boyfriend. Predictably the story ends with older sister and ex-boyfriend falling in love, and younger sister, through the power of 'love', converting drug-taker and thus making him an acceptable romantic boyfriend.

With the exception of one of these texts (15), the girls in the stories come from stereotypical families and have stereotypical hobbies and interests. The mothers' roles in all of the titles are not always mentioned, but when they are, less than half of the mothers work, even part time, outside of the home. The jobs that are mentioned for mothers are nurse (6), library assistant (10), union organiser (12), migrant women's resource centre worker (15), and partner in the family shop (16). Two mothers are students (15 and 18), and in the second of these stories, the daughter bitterly resents how little time her mother has for her now that she's a student. Four of the mothers are unambiguously located as full-time home people (1, 2, 5 and 14), and one of these is the classic, wicked, 'young' stepmother (2). While fathers may sometimes be found organising the evening meal (4 and 7), mothers are typically in the kitchen for the basic food preparation: cooking and serving breakfasts (8), baking biscuits and cakes to take on holiday (5), stewing peaches (13), cooking and freezing a week's evening meals (4). Fathers read the financial pages (1), go fishing (5), play golf (2), develop a new business (8), supervise at a factory (12), work 'too hard' (14), get promoted (18), become infatuated by younger women (2 and 17), or are absent-minded professors (17).

While romance heroes in these books often drive cars, the girls always get driven, or walk, or ride bikes. In the sporting field, girls are similarly stereotyped. Apart from one girl who becomes a top windsurfer (7), few others are sports-minded. One ice skates moderately well (once her new boyfriend teaches her) (12), one is a good gymnast (13), and one a champion swimmer (9). The girls are more frequently associated with the arts, the stereotypical field for romance. They are in school musicals (3 and 16), sing and play in rock bands (12), learn ballet and play the piano (13), and write for the school newspaper (4). Girls in these romances sometimes find that boyfriends resent the time they want to give to their hobbies or sport (12, 15)—although girlfriends are very understanding about the time boyfriends need for similar interests (1, 4, 7, 8, 13, 16, 18). Unless boyfriends become committed, or are already committed, to the same hobby as the girl—as eventually happens in numbers 9, 12 and 15—the romance flounders and the girl worries that perhaps she should forgo her non-romantic interest (numbers 12, 13, 15).

The girls spend most of their time talking to their friends, or planning what to wear, or what to say, in their next encounter with a boy. They are usually not doing well at school, and through the course of the novel, generally do less well because of the time they spend on their romantic plans. Conflicts with teachers and parents about homework not done or done badly are frequent features of the books (1, 3, 12, 13, 18). Typically the girl 'in love' cannot be rational and logical about her work—she daydreams, cries, locks herself in her room, or goes out to talk to her female friend. Being 'in love' causes a noticeable change in a girl's life:

> She *was* moody these days. Was love always like this? (no. 9: p. 81)

> My brain felt like scrambled eggs and I couldn't think about my problems any more today. Because of my ups and downs (mostly downs), I hadn't been keeping up with my homework...(no. 2: p. 90)

While she might initially resist 'love'—

> ...falling in love is the pits. Whenever anyone falls in love, their brain seems to turn to mush and their conversation becomes as boring as the magazines in a dentist's waiting room. (no. 4: p. 2)

—she finds that it's inevitable:

> ...I really thought I must be immune to it. And now—well, they say that things like measles and mumps affect you worse if you catch them later in life. Maybe that's why this love virus feels so horrible.'
> 'No, it's always horrible,' said Marie...'Half the time you're up in the air, and the other half of the time you're really down. That's just the way it is.' (no. 4: p. 8)

Only a few of the girls have part-time jobs, and the money they earn is for 'make-over' jobs. In *The Look of Love* (No. 1) Clarinda realises that without money 'the look of love' will not be possible:

> What did she need to turn herself into a new person? Money! Money for makeup and clothes and heaps of other things. Her elation faltered as she checked the contents of her piggy bank...She had never had any use for money. She didn't rush out buying records, or cosmetics or clothes... (pp. 9–10)

But she is about to. Fortunately Clarinda has one marketable skill: she is good at schoolwork. She begins a tutoring service, and when that doesn't provide quite enough money, she sells her schoolbooks:

> She sacrificed her biology, geography, and one of her favourite poetry books to the secondhand shop. This gave her enough money for the mascara she wanted, and the layby on her first pair of jeans. (p. 16)

In this particular novel, the heroine throws out her glasses, bleaches her hair, removes her orthodontic band, sheds fatty kilos, buys stretch jeans and mascara, and pretends she is not clever, in the metamorphosis from girlhood to romantic femininity. Blind, blonde and dumb, she then conforms more closely to what have seemed to her to be acceptable images of teenage femininity.

Careers, and life after school, are mentioned much more frequently for the boys in these stories, than for the girls. While boys curtail their social time because of their study (1, 3, 13, 16), or because they need to train for their professional sport commitments (7, 9, 18), girls just get hopelessly muddled trying to balance even their romance plans with their school homework, and seldom have any long-term plans. Even the school dux (1), or the champion windsurfer (7), or the school swimming star (9), or the top gymnast (13), aren't career-focussed. Girls typically don't think a great deal about their career options—there's too much distraction from romance. Take this particular example from number 5:

'What options are you doing at school next year?' he asked as his hand circled her shoulder blades. Jilly hadn't really thought about it. It felt good having him stroke the cream into her skin. Choosing options was the last thing on her mind.
'I don't know,' she said. 'Maybe...astronomy.'
She sounded as though she was asking a question.
'Astronomy!' said Tom. 'I didn't know they were offering it. That'd be great. You know, there was an explosion up there in one of the galaxies hundreds of years ago. It left a black hole.'
'A black hole? What's that got to do with horoscopes?'
'Horoscopes? Oh, you mean astrology.'
'Astrology, astronomy, what's the difference?' (p. 72)

Only two of the stories suggest that the girls have plans beyond the kiss. In *She's Got the Beat* (12), Niva hopes to continue playing music with her boyfriend in a rock band; and in *Designs on You* (15), Helen is actually working in a city boutique near where one of her boyfriends lives, and enjoying it. By comparison, boys in these stories are off on four-wheel drive trips across Australia (16); are computer experts (13); are fashion photographers (15); are studying to be veterinarians (13); or are aiming to be professional windsurfers (7), athletes (18), doctors (16), lawyers (18), or aeronautic engineers (5).

Boys know what they want, and they also know what girls want, consequently boys frequently play a significant role in the narrative's twist. For instance, they can actually help the girl construct her new image (3); they can tutor her when she falls behind at her schoolwork (1 and 3); they can do her assignments for her (13); they can save her from irresponsible boys (10 and 14); they can rescue her part-time job from failure (18); they can force her to keep up her training for a school swimming carnival (9). And many of the boys who will play the dominant roles are the 'old faithfuls' who have been part of the family scene for some time. They are the boys next door (1, 3, 13), or friends of the family (5, 7, 14, 16, 17), boys who know the girls for their true worth, and are comfortable in the family setting. They present as possible and suitable husbands.

Given these scenarios, it is rather difficult to see *Dolly Fiction* as a dynamic new series responding to the needs of women in the 1990s. Belinda Byrne's claim in her circular that 'We're talking positive role models here' is quite a peculiar statement in light of the dominant trend of the first eighteen novels in the series. Only one of the novels concludes with the heroine unpartnered, and even in this novel, the story ends with her contemplating which boy to choose (no. 15). This same novel is the only one to offer faintly positive roles for adult women, and the only one to present a young woman living alone with her mother. The novels unrelentingly portray images of adolescent femininity which tie girls to romantic inscription of their bodies for male approval; to complete absorption in the business of acquiring, preparing for and going on dates with boys; to reliance on male support, advice and financial backing; to disinterest in pursuing independent hobbies, sport, study, or career options. Becoming feminine—becoming romantic—means recognising that there will be inevitable tension in pursuing independence, and that it might be best to find a 'good guy' who'll give you the best options *within this framework*, so that lost opportunities and forsaken goals are less keenly felt.

Reading the romance

While it is relatively straightforward to consider the textual construction of romantic ideology in a series like *Dolly Fiction*, the possible effect of romance reading upon young women has always been contentious, and the argument has rightly been put that studies which recognise the 'complex relationships between social context, reader and text' (Taylor, 1989a) are urgently needed. Two such studies—one by John Willinsky and Mark Hunniford in Canada (1986), and another by Maylyn Lam in Australia (1986)—go some of the way towards exploring these 'complex relationships'. Both of these studies investigated pre-teen and teen romance readers who were identified by school reading surveys, and both offer examples of the ways in which these readers—all of them young women—make sense of their romance reading.

A major problem with studies of this nature is that young women have learned a great deal about what counts as a 'response' to a book, and what counts as fiction, and studies which attempt to unpack statements about response must take this discursive positioning into account. There are recognisable ways of talking about books; there are recognisable sets of assumptions about what constitutes a story; and, currently, as we argued in chapter 2, there is a recognisable emphasis in language and literature teaching which claims to value the 'personal' response of a reader to a text.

As we have argued earlier, reading is not an idiosyncratic activity: reading is learned. Romance fiction is therefore 'readable', because its generic conventions are recognisable and familiar. Series novels, in particular, rely upon instant recognition of the genre. They hold out the promise of more of the same, the series title acting as a brand name guaranteeing the quality. Readers are thus actively discouraged from making idiosyncratic meaning from the texts. These are not 'open' texts which offer space for textual play. Formula novels must appeal quickly and easily to thousands of readers, and, like franchised fast food, must not disappoint. Consequently the possibility of a multiplicity of responses is undesirable because it makes the success of the series less predictable. Interesting evidence of this was described in Radway's account of how the romance bookseller/guide in her study had to show her romance readers how to read particular texts which threatened to break out of the conventions of the typical romance genre (Radway, 1984: pp. 63–4). Once readers are positioned to accept—and to desire—romance ideology, particular textual conventions are usually quickly recognised.

Studies that have been made of young romance readers do offer interesting material about the ways in which young women talk about their readings of romance fiction. The Canadian study by Willinsky and Hunniford, for instance, largely replicated—with 42 grade 7 girls from a lower middle-class neighbourhood—Janice Radway's work with adult romance readers (1984). But Willinsky and Hunniford found significant differences between the ways in which the young women and the older women claimed to make use of the romances and talked about their romance reading. Willinsky and Hunniford claimed that the young readers were 'on the verge of a total surrender on a number of counts'; they were 'taking more from the books than the adults, more than many of us in education would want to ask' (1986: p. 21). When the girls completed a questionnaire listing reasons for reading romances, the statements 'because I wish I had a romance like the heroine's', and 'because I like to read about the strong, virile heroes' were scored as the two most important reasons for reading. This was quite different from the older women's responses, where 'for simple relaxation' and 'because reading is just for me; it is my time' were key reasons. Interviews with the girls supported this emphasis. The books had, according to Willinsky and Hunniford, become a 'beginner's manual for ensuing adolescence' (p. 28). One might add that they serve more as manuals for ensuing femininity than for adolescence.

Maylyn Lam's work with 42 older working-class and middle-class girls in an Australian high school (1986) indicates, however, a less complete acceptance by these girls of the world presented by romance fiction. While many of these older girls were still firm romance readers, they could feel the disjuncture between romance novels and the 'everyday reality' of their lives more keenly. One of the groups of girls Lam interviewed had stopped reading romance, and this group of ex-romance readers suggested in interview that this was largely because they no longer wanted to subject themselves to the pain of the disjuncture. However, other young women in Lam's study continued to enjoy the romance formula. The books still seemed 'real' and 'compelling' to many of them, largely because, Lam suggests, they were offering 'a view of the world in which feelings are of paramount importance' (1986: p. 44), a view of the world which Lam suggests is a crucial perspective for young women.

Like the younger readers, these fourteen and fifteen-year-olds observed the lessons in love and relationships offered through the novels—and enjoyed this focus in the texts—while becoming increasingly aware that the world of the romance was not their own world. Lam's comments at the end of her study indicate something of this dilemma for the older readers.

The Banyule readers' reflections on how and why romance fiction appeals to them defies the attempt to pigeonhole their responses into a theoretical framework. The girls do not articulate an awareness of 'the ideology of romance', but are quite capable of advancing a critique of the literary, social and sexual content of the novels. They are aware of differences between the boys they know and the fictional heroes who inhabit the *Sweet Valley* world. They are able to define ways in which the novels make them feel envious and inadequate, and are quite conscious of the low social status that is attached to their reading preferences. Yet they continue to read romances, reporting a degree of emotional involvement which is no less intense for the ambivalent nature of the pleasures that the books offer. (1986: p. 56)

Why girls continue to read romance, and to claim an 'emotional involvement' with such generically ritualistic novels, is, of course, the key question. And to add a rather different perspective to this question, it can be considered from another angle. Given that reading practices are learned and reading positions are adopted, why is it that some girls have learned reading practices and adopted reading positions which reject the stereotypes offered through romance fiction? How differently positioned are these girls who are *not* romance readers from those who are, and how might alternative positioning facilitate such learning? Are there other subject positions available to non-romance readers which make it easier to resist romance ideology as it is developed through formula fiction? And what might a study of such readers tell us about romance reading?

Social class membership has not been a key factor in the studies by Willinsky and Hunniford, Lam or Christian-Smith, but it could be argued that the lived social and cultural experiences of girls as members of oppressed and disadvantaged groups may be significant in positioning some girls more readily to adopt romance ideology—and to accept romance fiction—as the most promising method of resolving the contradictions of becoming feminine. For instance Taylor's work with an inner city group of Australian girls found that those who came from non-English speaking backgrounds were more attracted by romance fiction than were the other girls in the class (Taylor, 1989a).

Given this interest in the possible influence of social and cultural experiences on the construction of romance readers, we did undertake a small-scale study of a group of girls who are not normally romance readers, but who saw themselves as 'readers', and were keen to read a new attractively packaged series of romance fiction. A neighbourhood group of three girls aged eleven to thirteen was well-known to one of us. The girls all come from middle-class family backgrounds, their parents have university educations and professional occupations, and the girls are all seen to be successful at school. The lived experiences of these girls were experiences of privilege—all of them had professional career aspirations and expectations of economic security.

With this background for the girls, we wondered what would be their interest in reading a new romance series like *Dolly Fiction*, and what their reaction to such a series might be. The girls were asked if they would like to read books from a new romance series. While all of the girls had read some formula romance novels before, and had clear textual expectations of such books, the girls did not call themselves 'romance readers'. They liked a wide variety of material— adventure, mystery, science fiction, historical romance, fantasy. However, when they were shown the first eighteen of the brand new *Dolly Fiction* series, they were happy to read them. *Dolly* magazine is very popular with girls of this age, and the link from the fiction to the magazine was obviously attractive. While none of these girls actually bought *Dolly* magazine, some of their friends did, and they had also been able to borrow copies from the municipal library.

The girls were asked to read as many of the novels as they wanted, to keep a journal of anything they wished to note about the books, and then to talk to the researcher afterwards about their reading (the researcher was a well known and familiar adult to the girls). Initially the girls were asked as a group to select which of the eighteen they most wanted to read, and their discussions were taped.

Typically they used the back cover text, and the inside front cover extract to help them choose. One of the girls picked up the word play of several of the titles immediately, and all three seemed discerning in their selection. They seemed to know what they expected to like, and all rejected several titles immediately. They were after books that had a good 'storyline':

This looks like it might be OK. Not so soppy.

Perhaps this one might be a mystery . . .

This's got a different kind of twist . . .

They wanted books that were not what they considered to be 'typical romances', and one that they all seized upon as having potential was no. 11, *First Impressions*. *First Impressions* is not the usual romance, in that it is predominantly written from the viewpoint of the hero, Jack Darcy. However at the beginning of the book a page reads:

WARNING!
Before you start to read this book, I reckon you ought to know what you're letting yourself in for. They say it's girls who are interested in reading about romance—but this story is written by a guy. And Jack Darcy's no ordinary guy, either. . .Just so you don't get stuck with Jack all the time, I'm going to add my own comments at the end of every chapter, to make sure you get a girl's point of view as well. Happy reading!
SIGNED
Liz Bennet

One other book in the first eighteen of this series was constructed like this. The rest were all ostensibly from the single viewpoint: the viewpoint of, as we noted earlier in this chapter, a girl who is usually not doing well at school, typically not able to organise her school, social and family life into any tolerable order, and often not confident in her own ability to be interesting or attractive to boys. For most of these girls the greatest crisis in their lives is likely to be what they'll wear to the disco, or whether they'll get a glimpse of their boyfriend at school before lunch. They are not, as Knodel suggested (1982), protagonists for some girls to admire. Consequently a romance book which purports to be from a male perspective seems to offer not only a novel narrative twist, but also a more valued, because more valuable, perspective. *First Impressions* suggests that it could be a male discourse about romance, a discourse which many women would see as potentially enlightening but also potentially unusual, interesting and more powerful. As one of the girls said, 'I know what girls think. I want to know what a guy thinks'. This has also been an emphasis in *Dolly* magazine, which runs a 'Boys On' feature every month, purporting to offer what boys have to say about a set issue, for example 'Casual Sex' (July, 1989), and 'Girlfriends' (August, 1989).

The girls followed different patterns as they read the books. One of the three—the youngest—read thirteen of the possible eighteen in the two-week holiday period, but the other two lost interest fairly quickly. One read five of the books, and one four. The older girls seemed to complete as many as they did out of a sense of duty to the researcher. Their journal entries were short and not always complete. Both of the older girls apologetically explained that they had a number of other books that they had wanted to read.

The youngest girl stopped on her thirteenth book, and didn't want any more. However, she said that she had quite liked the *Dolly Fiction*. One, in particular, had been very interesting to her, and she was quite surprised, and a little dismayed at her enjoyment of the book:

> I thought about this and thought—oh, how embarrassing—I actually got hooked into a romance book...

This devaluing of romance fiction had been a strong feature of all the girls' responses. None of them really wanted to like romance fiction. All of them assumed that the researcher and their parents thought such books were 'trash' or 'pathetic', and when asked why parents wouldn't like the books, the girls offered reasons like:

> Dad doesn't mind what I read, although he would think that reading stuff like this was a bit silly. He wouldn't understand why on earth I'd want to read books like that...

> The girls in the stories are just so pathetic...

> Mum says that whatever goes into your head has to come out in some way, so why fill it up with junk?

> The parents in the books are often stupid old bats yelling at each other and so on...My family's not like that.

They also described how boys devalued romance novels:

> Boys wouldn't be interested, because of the reputation they've got. Because girls read them.

> Boys wouldn't like to read books like this. Think it's sissy to like books and romance and everything like that.

When asked what they thought about the possibility of working with romance fiction like *Dolly Fiction* in the mixed-sex classroom, all the girls were adamant that it would be a mistake. They argued that they wanted the opportunity to study other books at school, and they claimed that while some girls might appreciate the chance of working with books they knew and liked, this would be more than offset by the likely reaction of the boys. They were sure that boys would hate the novels, and laugh at their use. When pressured about what sort of girls preferred romance fiction, one of the girls suggested that such girls were probably a bit 'boy-crazy', but it was more than likely that they didn't really enjoy reading very much:

...these give them more satisfaction than other books. It's the girls that don't read much that read them. Because they don't want to go down into a long novel or anything but this is about something they might know something about. They think it's nice. I guess at school—maybe this isn't right—you're sort of considered a square if you're reading long novels but if you're reading these, people don't mind. This isn't like a proper fiction.

Romance reading may be seen, at least by some students, as a resistance to school authorised material—to institutionalised schooling—and research by Christian-Smith (1987) and Lam (1986), would seem to support this claim. But for these non-romance readers such reading was largely a waste of time:

It's a waste of reading.

You start talking about what's in these books. Speak like them. Act like them. Write like them and stuff like that. You start to think that everything's going to end up happily as soon as you meet the right person. Or who they think the right person is for them.

If you take this stuff seriously, if you think, 'Oh, this could be me', I think it could go a bit far and you could live in a world that isn't real. Some girls might think that —if they were stupid...Guys just aren't like that. This is so unreal.

As with Taylor's work (1989a), this 'unreality' of the books was a major, and quite unsolicited, focus of the girl's discussion. If the girls could not position themselves to accept and be seduced by the *fantasy* of the romance, then the other more obvious reading position to take up was that of the *reality* of the romance text.

They're supposed to be about real life but they're not like real life. It's about real life and they're making it *not* life.

Falling in love does happen but not like that...

No way are they realistic. Nothing ever happens like this...All these spunky guys. Guys just aren't like that. They're just so unreal in appearance.

Yet the girls could see that in part it was the 'unreality'—the 'fantasy'—that was attractive to many of the readers who were romance fans.

Some girls...don't have boyfriends and they just like reading books instead of having the real thing.

The girls noticed how different the *Dolly Fiction* series was from other books that they had read, and how the series fared badly by comparison. One of the girls in particular was able to speculate about what generally made other books more interesting:

> Other books are about adventure and mystery. These are all romance. They're pretty boring. You don't want romance to be the main part of your life. Of course it's got to be a big part because you've got to get married and everything, but there's all the school part and just having fun and lots of books just about school life aren't just about romance. I like other books better because with these you know what's going to happen. With the others you don't...I like books that are about people my age. They don't really happen in real life. Fantasy books don't have any real life, but they make you feel as if it could be real life. With these, you suddenly meet the guy and you marry them—but it doesn't happen like that.

The girls were also critical of the way the romance books were written, and had much to say about the construction of the books. They commented upon their readability levels:

> They're all about older people and yet it sounds like they're written for younger people.

Their narrative style:

> These have all different people, but they're put together in the same way all the time...They're very direct, like they always say, 'She felt this', or, 'She said this'. Other books tell you what they want to tell you, but they say it in an interesting way. They use more description. Much more interesting to sit down and read. These—you only keep reading to find out what happens at the end. With novels you also do that but you also enjoy reading them while you're reading them. They're much more artistically written if you know what I mean.

Their character framing:

> The heroes usually know everything. They've just got to sort their girls out. The girls are all sort of mixed up. The man next to them helps them sort it out. They're all the same. The boys are really nice and intelligent and the girls are kissing their feet sort of.

Their stylistic artistry:

> It's pathetic how they describe things, like, I wrote this one down: 'Tingling vibrations of electric currents racing through her body'. Pathetic. And there's all these exclamations. In one paragraph. Just listen...

The proofing and editing accuracy of the production:

> There's so many terrible spelling and typing mistakes. It's awful. They've even got the guy's name wrong in this one.

These three girls are, we would suggest, differently positioned as readers than are many other girls. Their class and family backgrounds have encouraged the perception that romance is a devalued genre, both as a popular art form, and as a source of information about adolescent girls. And this matters to them. They are ready to link up with, at least at this stage of their lives, their parents and their teachers and to take up subject positions that seem to offer more authority. While versions of romance ideology may well be more attractive to them at different points in their lives, when they are differently positioned discursively, at this stage they perceive of infinitely more options than the world of *Dolly Fiction* offers. They will not easily take up the gendered subject positions that romance ideology constructs.

In addition, they want something else out of reading than romance fiction will give them. They like to read other books, because they have varied and extensive intertextual experiences. They are able to be discerning about what they want in fiction, and for them, this romance series was, on the whole, badly written, badly produced, boring and trite. They framed the series immediately—even before they had read any of the books—into a generic type which led them to anticipate particular textual and ideological conventions. And these conventions were drawn from discourses about success, schooling, marriage and adolescence which these three girls rejected. They did not connect with their lived experiences as privileged and successful middle-class girls. The texts could not appeal to them as a guide to teen relationships and adolescence, and yet once the fantasy of the texts was rejected, that was the only other dominant reading frame to adopt. As a guide to adolescent femininity, the series was unattractive. As young adult literature, it was also unattractive.

Girls and women know that romances are fiction: they are fantastic, unreal, impossible. But it is this unreality which many girls and women find seductive. While schools may not be able to alter significantly the discursive positioning of many young women, schools can offer approaches to working with texts which make it easier to recognise the constructed nature of texts, and which can begin the process of showing women ways in which they might reposition themselves discursively. It should not be surprising to us, for instance, that year 7 girls like those in Willinsky and Hunniford's study are still slightly confused about the textual construction of 'reality', but it should be a matter of some concern if older students were not able to examine ways in which texts construct different versions of reality, and to ask why this is possible. The question of what reality is constructed in literature is a key one, and in chapter 2 we examined some of the concerns that feminist aesthetics has had with just this issue. As we argued there, we learn how to read texts, because we learn to take up various subject positions which allow the text to be framed in specific ways. The way in which some girls have already accepted romance fantasies as an apparent solution to the 'problem' of becoming a woman—a lover, a wife, a mother—positions them more readily to accept romance fiction as a discourse of relevance and interest.

If formula romance fiction does discursively belong to patriarchal systems of organising and defining reality, it should be a matter of concern to us that the genres are so attractive to certain groups of women. Why, for instance, do some women reject the subject positions formula romance fiction offers, and why are other women apparently seduced by them? Part of the answer to this must lie in the different discursive positions women can adopt in relation to romance texts. The lived experiences of some girls, as oppressed and marginalised groups, partially accounts for their willingness to accept romance ideology as an alternative solution to the patriarchal parameters of their present and future lives. But the representations of romance ideology in formula novels do offer the possibility of textually exploring these parameters in tangible form. Such an exploration will be more easily undertaken if girls' textual experiences are rich—if they have read of other ways to construct women's futures, and of other ways to speak of love. And if they have some understanding of the way in which language practices are social and cultural processes.

We accept that romance fiction, like many other popular cultural texts, connects strongly with some young women's lives, and we accept that there is a complex interplay between girls' conscious and unconscious desires which popular culture, through its powerful sets of interconnected images, links with. Fashioning the feminine in our society is big business, and it is unquestionably the dominant contemporary discourse influencing the construction of female subjectivity. But it is not the only discourse, and much of what this book argues for is that discourses 'not intended for her' (Rich, 1980: p. 243)—discourses not offering women speaking positions of authority —be replaced by others.

Romance ideology is not a discourse intended for 'her'. It is a discourse which locks women into passive and submissive response rather than active and independent action; a discourse which cannot construct a future for women without men; a discourse which necessitates the humiliating and crippling romantic inscription of the body. Romantic ideology operates through fairy tales and comics, through movies and television soaps, through magazines and commercial advertisements, to construct women's conscious and unconscious desires for love, for difference, for escape, for security, for sensuality in an apparently natural and inevitable way. The result is, as Ann Snitow (1984: p. 265) has argued so persuasively, that:

> When women try to picture excitement, the society offers them one vision, romance. When women try to imagine companionship, the society offers them one vision, male, sexual companionship. When women try to fantasize about success, mastery, the society offers them one vision, the power to attract a man. When women try to fantasize about sex, the society offers them taboos on most of its imaginable expressions except those that deal directly with arousing and satisfying men. When women try to project a unique self, the society offers them very few attractive images. True completion for women is nearly always presented as social, domestic, sexual.

Formula romance novels should not be protected from scrutiny because they are popular culture, nor because they are fiction, nor because they are specially written for women and give women pleasure. They do not grow out of discourses which serve women well. They grow out of consumer-oriented discourses which have vested interests in constructing groups of women as identifiable and therefore commercially marketable; and they grow out of patriarchal discourses which depend upon the continuation of unequal heterosexual couplings and domestic labour.

5

Dear diary: girls and writing

Boys are more to do with practical work and experiments and girls are more to learn and listen and enjoy writing. (A schoolboy, quoted in White, 1986: p. 572)

Girls in their writing demonstrate that they are children, thereby earning the approval of their teachers, while boys are boys and, as such, are suspect and troublesome in this ideological world. But the world of...school is of limited duration: beyond it is the world of work and leisure. (Poynton, 1985: p. 36)

Chapter 2 indicated how complex were some of the issues associated with girls and writing, and in this chapter we will attempt to unravel some of this complexity. As the schoolboy quoted above claims, girls have traditionally been linked with writing (and traditionally been regarded as good at writing), and Janet White's report on national writing testing in the UK (1986) confirms that these assumptions have a certain validity. Her work refers to intensive testing of children from England, Wales and Northern Ireland since 1979, in relation to girls' and boys' attitudes to writing and to their different abilities with school writing tasks. From that work she makes the claim that 'in each of the surveys conducted, on all of the analytic criteria used, girls have been found to achieve higher mean scores than boys' (p. 563). She also notes that 'at the end of primary schooling, girls not only have achieved a soundly based competency in written work, but their sense of themselves as writers is similarly robust' (p. 565).

This is not the case, however, for boys. White notes the 'pervasiveness of an attitude that writing doesn't matter for boys' (p. 565), and one could also note here the claim made by

Jane Begos (1987) who, in a study of female diarists, noted the absence of diaries written by young men. Begos looked for explanations for this in different attitudes held by adolescent girls and boys to writing. She saw female diary writing as being consistent with a general trend linking women to writing, and argued that historically it has been women who have maintained familial communication links; women who have kept up extensive correspondence and produced the diaries and memoirs which frequently serve as 'the genealogical and historical records for the family' (Begos, 1987: p. 69).

But it is men who are generally regarded as being the writers of philosophy, psychology, science, history, poetry and drama. Control of the more powerful discourses lies with men; the lower status written forms—the service industry of writing such as secretarial work, family letter-writing, diary entries, genealogical records, novel writing—are the ones dominated by women workers. Janet White (1986) comments on how few women have pursued careers in writing-related domains such as journalism and editing to the 'point of visibility'. She notes that while women proliferate in magazine journalism, and amongst copy editors and editorial assistants, very few achieve promotion to top jobs. Even in the advertising industry, only one in six account executives and about one in five copy writers are women (1986: p. 562).

> Considering the disparity between women's early achievements in literacy and their subsequent paid employment, we need to ask why it is that thousands of able girl writers leave school and go into secretarial jobs, in the course of which they will patiently revise and type the semi-literate manuscripts of their male bosses, or else return in droves to the primary classroom, there to supervise the production of another generation of pen-wise girls. (White, 1986: p. 562)

Clearly one of the first paradoxes to note is that, despite the professed weighting society gives to literacy skills, being good at school writing apparently counts for little in the job market, and does not offer women speaking positions of authority in the more powerful public discourses. Rather obviously, writing competence does not lead directly to career prospects —neither careers in commercial writing-related fields like publishing or advertising, nor careers in professions like law or academia. And by scribbling quietly in corners, girls are perhaps further cutting off access to the more public yet masculinist worlds of science and technology. Writing is unquestionably a private and passive activity for most schoolchildren, and for girls, it may well operate as a form of escape from the more competitive and risky arenas dominated by boys.

However, some women educators do see potential in the writing classroom. A recent anthology edited by Cynthia Caywood and Gillian Overing (1987) claims that contemporary moves taken by writing pedagogy towards a 'process' rather than a 'product' orientation have been very important for women. Their argument is that:

> ...the process model, insofar as it facilitates and legitimizes the fullest expression of the individual voice, is compatible with the feminist revisioning of hierarchy, if not essential to it...The writing course has the potential to be the single most important learning experience for students if it provides them with confidence in their own ideas and belief in their own authority. (1987: pp. xiv–xv)

The anthology edited by Caywood and Overing brings together a number of different papers which offer practical advice for feminist teachers. But the anthology is premised on a clear assumption that personal expression (student's 'own authority') is something that can be fostered with the right classroom practice, and that once fostered, will be important for feminist practice. Our argument here has been that such practices have limited potential: they gloss the socially constructed nature of language practices and the discursive nature of subjectivity. Instead such pedagogical ideals assume that equality of opportunity is achieved by providing equality of access to language, and by offering sensitive and sympathetic readers and listeners to children's language. While both of these qualities are of obvious importance in the education of young women, we have argued that they will not be enough on their own. The rest of this chapter will try to indicate why, and will offer alternative approaches to the way in which texts may be 'read' and 'written' in the classroom.

The chapter will initially consider three questions about gender and literacy. How is *difference* between girls' and boys' texts read, and is such difference significant for feminist practice? Do many typical school writing tasks posit stereotypical gendered subject positions, and thus inadvertently support misogynistic attitudes? And are there other ways of approaching reading and writing in the classroom which might explore *difference* differently, by opening out other discursive positions from which to write and to read, and thus maximising the space available within the classroom for counter-hegemonic practice?

Girls' writing: boys' writing

In a description of the results of a large-scale study of Sydney primary school children's writing, Cate Poynton claims:

> Girls and boys write about different things almost from the start, with the difference increasing with age and the common ground becoming smaller. Girls write about home activities...dress and appearance, romance, and fantasy worlds inhabited by fairies, witches, characters from children's stories...commercial toys...and talking animals and objects. Boys write about playing or watching sport and other physical activities such as bike-racing...Boys' fantasy worlds are inhabited by creatures from outer space, assorted monsters (preferably of the kind that kill people unexpectedly and messily, with lots of blood), everyday burglars, kidnappers, and murderers—and when the writer himself is a character in an adventure story then he is usually accompanied by a group of his male class-mates...Boys also write about topics that do not lend themselves to 'story'-writing e.g. the solar system, dinosaurs, radios. (Poynton, 1985: pp. 34–5)

Poynton's observations are supported by other work which has looked at children's writing. For instance, Jane Romatowski and Mary Trepanier-Street (1987) analysed children's stories written by 180 elementary schoolchildren in grades 1 through 6 (90 boys and 90 girls) and noted the 'very strong male predominance in their stories'. They documented how all of the children constructed more male than female characters in their stories: how over 50 different occupational roles had been assigned to male characters, but only 12 (including such roles as princess, cook, nurse, and hula dancer) to female characters; and how high intensity action (e.g., climbing a mountain, escaping from danger), and problem solving were predominantly linked with male characters (Romatowski and Trepanier-Street, 1987: p. 18).

This study also noted how female writers more frequently assigned emotional states to their characters and more pro-social behaviours (such as helping, sharing, empathising) than did male writers, who by contrast frequently constructed characters who were verbally and physically aggressive. Romatowski and Trepanier-Street's work is supported by a study led by Dorothy Tuck (Tuck et al., 1985) which looked at the relationship between stereotyped characters and sex of the writer in children's work. Tuck's work concluded that children tended to create characters of their own sex in their stories, and that female and male authors both showed a similar tendency to stereotype their characters.

Approximately one-half of the characters created by female and male authors in Tuck's study were classified as stereotyped. However, the most revealing findings of the study came from a comparison of the prevalent traits of female and male characters. Whereas 74 per cent of the male characters exhibited assertive and persistent behaviour, only 23 per cent of the female characters exhibited these same characteristics (Tuck et al., 1985: p. 250). Tuck emphasises that the criteria for this trait required that a character win or succeed at a task through self-determination, perseverance, or, by overcoming fear, criteria that, as she claims, 'either sex should find desirable and appropriate in many situations' (p. 250). The fact that so few female authors employed these traits when creating female characters is telling, as is the fact that few male authors developed character traits associated either with sensitive and loving behaviour or the expression of emotions.

Apart from these very obvious differences in *character construction* in children's stories, differences in the *style of narrative* developed by children have also been commented upon. Poynton (1985) observed that 'girls produce single Complication Resolution structures, where boys have a preference for repetitive (serial) structures, which girls almost never produce' (p. 36). Janet White (1986) noted that:

> . . . while girls outnumber boys in preference for writing letters and stories (though narrative writing is the favoured activity for both sexes, and remains thus at age 15 also), boys' interests in writing tend to cluster around factual, episodic writing assignments. . . Girls are more inclined to enjoy writing about their family and personal experiences and to view the writing of poetry as something enjoyable in appropriate circumstances. (1986: p. 565)

In a study of the narratives of four older college-level students, Elizabeth Flynn (1988) makes similar claims for difference between female and male writing, but this time in respect to different sets of experiences. She argues that females and males do not use language in identical ways, or represent the world in a similar fashion, and her analysis of four first-year students' work offers some evidence of this difference. As Flynn claims from her 'readings' of the students' stories: 'The narratives of the female students are stories of interaction, of connection, or of frustrated connection. The narratives of the male students are stories of achievement, of separation, or of frustrated achievement' (1988: p. 428). Such readings are typical of approaches often adopted by feminist aesthetics, which has frequently adopted a similar standpoint about what it might mean to write about women's experiences from a woman's perspective (e.g., Flynn and Schweickart, 1986; Jacobus, 1979).

What could be concluded from these many studies of writing—at any level of institutionalised learning—is that there are noticeable differences both in the topics children choose to work with, the characters that female and male children construct for school stories, and the type of texts they prefer to construct. But the significance of this—in terms of it being a tangible textual demonstration of children's clear acceptance of the need to take up strongly stereotypical gendered subject positions—has not often been explored. Bronwyn Davies' work with pre-schoolers (1989) provides a very clear account of this process at work in the pre-school, but such studies are, on the whole, still rare. For the most part, what children actually write about (the speaking positions they take up and the subjects they so construct), seems not to be of key concern to many teachers. Indeed, as one English educator argues (Medway, 1987), language classrooms are often 'contentless' arenas—neither teachers nor researchers usually notice, for example, what the subject matter of children's writing is: '...while there is no shortage of schemes for categorising writing by rhetorical function, form and genre, I have found almost nothing which deals with what the writing is about ...(Medway, 1987: pp. 11–12). Peter Medway argues that writing for its own sake has become so important at school, that the subject matter of the writing classroom seems not to matter.

If this is so, it partly accounts for why so little attention has been given to the excessively stereotypical nature of much children's writing, and why so little pedagogical concern has been directed towards discursively placing the texts children construct. And yet Carolyn Steedman's (1982) analysis of a story constructed by three eight-year-old working-class girls— *The Tidy House*—indicates the possibilities offered by such 'different' readings. The girls' story, claims Steedman, can be seen to be about 'romantic love, marriage and sexual relations'; 'the desire of mothers for children and their resentment of them'; and 'the means by which those children are brought up to inhabit a social world' (p. 1). Readings like these by Steedman are thus able to demonstrate something of the way in which a group of eight-year-old girls struggles to reconcile the inevitable tensions and ambiguities of pre-teen femininity and class identity by trying out the various subject positions offered through narrative. The readings make it easier to understand what Steedman calls 'the huge mythologies of love and sex that inform our culture', as well as the way in which 'working class girls become working class women' (p. 12).

Gemma Moss's readings of adolescent girls' stories (Moss, 1989) raise similar possibilities, by exploring the space available to girls within popular fiction forms for the exploration of gendered identity. Moss's argument is that the sets of cultural knowledge that children use in their writing 'are not homogeneous but diverse and full of contradictions'. As a result, the meanings that can be established 'are multiple not unitary and are temporarily achieved, not permanently fixed' (p. 121). Moss reads the girls' stories for evidence of struggle— struggle to deal with dominant versions of masculinity and femininity, and struggle to find space within the conventions of popular fiction to write differently and more powerfully.

Such readings would be particularly helpful in primary school classrooms imbued with the heady discourse of student authorship and its emphasis on the publication of children's writing. Stereotypical children's texts—often more violently and blatantly stereotyped than commercially produced texts—are frequently authorised as classroom reading material. They are 'published' and put on display in classrooms so that children can read each other's work, and yet provision to discuss such texts—in terms of what the stereotypes indicate about the adoption of gendered subject positions—seems seldom to have been made.

Consider, for example, the following children's text: *Bloodbath Efa Bunnies.*

BLOODBATH EFA BUNNIES

One day our class wanted a war. They were prepared. They had M.60's on the louvres, pockets full of grenades.

One day an efa bunny came up the stairs. 5J decided to have fun, so they got all their M.60's and shot him. Then, from the hills and the rocks and from the dunnies, they were all heavily armed. But were we afraid? Were we scared?

'YES!' We were packin' it.

An efa bunny was being nice to Alice and gave her an efa egg with a grenade in it. Millions of efa bunnies were coming up the stairs and Carol took the jump and decked 'em. AAAAA! 'My God! Super blubber!' they said as they got up. They all said, 'Run!'

As they ran back to their fort screaming, Kyran got out his water pistol, and shot a bunny. But that didn't work. So he got out his pop gun and shot him again. Pop! But that didn't work. Then a wittle efa bunny shot him (right between the eyes). Code name Cam and code name Frem got out laser guns. Cameron shot his moonbeam laser and the ray rebounded off a brick wall and shot an efa bunny in the tum tum. Jane had an affair with the bunny that was fat, because he gave her an efa egg with arsenic and nitro-glycerine in it.

'Bang!' and Jane was never seen again.

'Good riddance,' said code name Cam.

James told some jokes to an efa bunny and bored him to death. Then Chris tried to do it and was shot instantly. Code name Cam ran up to the hills and code name Ly covered him. Cam, Ly and Frem were up to save the world.

Then code name Ly, code name Cam, and code name Frem said, 'Peace brother efa bunnies.'

While Helen was looking for eggs, an efa bunny was right behind her. The efa bunny said, 'HEY YOU!' and blew her away. It was a tragic death, but what have we been waiting for (music).

There was a line of efa bunnies out the front of the kindergarten. Adam took a bolt through the efa bunnies (music) but got killed. Russell and Sally were captured by the efa bunnies, taken to their fort and put in front of a firing squad, and while holding hands, were killed—brutally. Lawrence and Sophie wanted to make the most of their last moments together (music). The wedding was sabotaged by efa bunnies. Yay! Yay!

They killed everybody at that wedding. Charmaine said to John, 'I love...', but an efa bunny had different ideas and then he branded them with bullets.

A squad of efa bunnies came upstairs. They grabbed Kevin and put him on a fire and the efa bunnies made these noises (music). When he was cooked enough, they took him out and chopped his tongue off and gave him to the bears. But the bears couldn't stand him and his tongue. They made A La De Tongue soup.

Sophie and Sally went to the efa bunny dentist and the dentist ripped all their teeth out and made a necklace out of their teeth. Sophie ran, but the efa bunnies caught her and they crucified her.

Code name Frem, code name Cam, code name Ly, code name Si, and code name Dan escaped from the efa bunnies.

THE END
(TRUE STORY)

This text was collected from a year 5 class in a provincial Australian primary school, as part of a study of the writing completed by the class over a year. Two nine-year-old boys intially worked together in class for several days as they constructed this story, but they were later joined by two other boys and the foursome stayed together over several weeks in the drafting of the collaborative tale. The story's name originated from a spate of classroom 'efa bunny' jokes (a lisping

Easter bunny) common at that time of the year (April). In the story, the four student writers—plus an additional male friend—attempt to ward off an attack on their class by efa bunnies laden down with grenades, 'M60's', and an assortment of other artillery. Anzac comradeship and Rambo individualism are intertwined as the boys cover their mates, shoot moonbeam lasers that rebound with deadly accuracy, and eventually 'save the world'. Two groups of protagonists are clearly defined in the narrative: the *real* boys, and the 'other' —in this case, the girls and the non-real non-masculine boys. And it is the *real* boys who assume the right to speak with authority, to construct the 'other' as gendered spoken subjects.

Of the nine girls in the class, all are mentioned by name except for two—an Asian girl, and a new girl who had been in the class only a few weeks. Of the seven girls referred to in the story, six are destroyed, and in ugly ways. They are blown up by grenades, killed by a firing squad, 'branded by bullets', or crucified. But before they are eliminated, the girls are given reasonably stereotypical roles. Four of the girls are identified by their relationships with boys: having 'affairs', holding hands with boys, getting married, saying 'I love...' Another two are given similarly ineffectual roles in this war story. While the boys ward off the enemy during the war, the girls search for Easter eggs.

The only girl who is not killed, not married off, and not day-dreaming of Easter eggs, is the biggest girl in the class (all are identified by their real names in this story, and note the final line: THE END—A TRUE STORY). The big girl very early in the story jumps on top of marauding efa bunnies and 'decks 'em': ' "AAAAA! My God! Super Blubber!" they said as they got up. They all said, "Run!" ' No need to kill off this female: her size and aggression have effectively excluded her anyway. (What worse fate for a girl than to be called 'Super Blubber'?) The non-macho group of boys in the story receive similar fates to the girls and are identified in one of two ways: either they are involved with the girls (holding hands, getting married and so on), or they have drawn attention to themselves as non-active and non-physical: 'James told some jokes to an efa bunny and bored him to death. Then Chris tried to do it and was shot instantly...A squad of efa bunnies... grabbed Kevin and put him on a fire and...took him out and chopped his tongue off and gave him to the bears. But the bears couldn't stand him and his tongue. They made A La De Tongue soup.'

This story is typical of the style of boys' narratives Poynton identified (1985), and the characters typical of those described by Tuck et al. (1985) and Romatowski and Trepanier-Street (1987). It is not unusual. Stories like this abound in classrooms and serve to indicate—quite dramatically—the power boys take, and are allowed to take, in schools (see Baker and Davies, 1989, for a discussion of classroom interaction in this regard). The topic that this group chose to write about challenged the teacher's role as moral guardian and as disciplinarian—and won. The teacher did not comment publicly to the boys about the content of their story, nor try to prevent its publication, and the authors were aggressively confident and brash in the classroom during its production. The fact that this story was 'published'—that is, typed, placed in cardboard covers and added to the classroom library of children's stories—confirms for the girls (and the other group of boys) the gendered reality of the classroom. It indicates to them that misogynistic, violent attacks like this are seen to be humorous and acceptable, and that even a seemingly power-less group of nine-year old school boys has the right—because it can take up speaking positions of authority—to mock and abuse girls and other boys in this way. The class members named in the story did not confront their teacher or the 'authors' of the story. However one week after the story had been placed in the classroom on public display, it had disappeared. Someone—or some group—decided to operate upon their own sense of indignation and humiliation.

Writing tasks and topics: the potential for misogyny

This particular classroom incident became possible because the publication of this story was not really very different from a number of other misogynistic and stereotypical classroom practices. The reality of much classroom life—a reality partially constructed by and continually reinforced by many textual practices, including the production, selection and use of class-room reading materials—is that the failure to identify with a stereotypical gendered subjectivity can lead to humiliation and mockery from other students, and indirect (sometimes direct) pressure from teachers to conform. (See, for instance, the classroom transcript analysed in Baker and Davies, 1989, and the teacher comments on pupils noted in Clarricoates, 1978 and Stanworth, 1984.) The accepted—authorised—world of the classroom is a world largely composed of stereotypes: in books, in classroom talk, in playground behaviour, in acceptable dress, in extracurricular activities. And not surprisingly the conventions of many of the common written genres endorsed for classroom use also rely upon many of these same gender stereotypes. They do not posit reading and writing positions of authority for young women. Similarly subject matter authorised for the classroom—the subject matter authorised through commercial mass publication of 'books for children'—offers few opportunities to challenge the stereotypes and posit speaking positions of more authority for young women.

Gendered genres

> Telling fairy stories, even telling good fairy stories very well. . .simply doesn't count. The positions of real power and influence in our society necessitate command of genres for which boys' educational experience provides an appropriate preparation and girls' doesn't. Even in terms of the written genre of most significance in secondary and most tertiary education—exposition. . .—girls' genre competence at primary school is not merely irrelevant but positively disabling. (Poynton, 1985: p. 36)

While the debate about genre and the teaching of writing is, as we considered in chapter 2, complex and quite difficult to untangle, what does seem clear is that certain genre forms predominate in classrooms, and that both children and teachers have preferences for (or take up) some rather than others (Martin and Rothery, 1984; White, 1986). Poynton's claim that some genre forms are potentially more powerful and more useful than others is thus a key question to raise in connection with girls and writing, if, as it has been claimed, the forms of writing that girls become 'good' at are not the forms of writing that will ultimately be useful in terms of careers or employment.

But there is also another question to consider. Is there some intrinsic value in writing stories or poems or letters—in taking up speaking positions in these discourses—which, although they are not part of the masculine domain of work and realism, have potential power for young women? In other words, should forms of writing that are not masculinist in orientation be actively encouraged as part of a feminist pedagogy? Flynn argues that they should, and cites Adrienne Rich when she warns 'of the dangers of immasculation, of identifying against oneself and learning to think like a man' (1988: p. 433). She emphasises 'the importance of critical activity on the part of the woman student—refusing to accept the givens of our culture, making connections between facts and ideas which men have left unconnected' (pp. 433–4). Thinking as a woman is to involve 'active construction, the recreation of one's identity'. Identities may not be so easily known—and in this book we have argued that they are constantly struggled over and imperfectly known—but Flynn's argument that women must refuse to accept the *givens* of our culture is important.

Language, as the ebb and flow of our day-to-day existence, too easily passes as a 'given', as a neutral message system, as an almost transparent medium through which we communicate. We tend to forget that some things are much more easily—and apparently more 'naturally'—said and therefore 'known' than others. This is not because some words and phrases are more appropriate, or more accurate, or more truthful, or even more obvious. It is because the discursive conventions of generic forms have become so familiar that they then seem natural, commonsensical, and therefore 'right'. This was made clear to one of us in a small research study completed with student teachers who were studying children's literature (Gilbert, 1985).

The students were introduced to sexist stereotypes in children's stories, and yet at the end of the course, when they constructed their own children's stories, the students relied on many of those same stereotypes to build their narratives. In discussion about the sexism in their stories, students made these remarks:

> It somehow seemed wrong to have the animals being mean to a little girl wombat.

> It was easier to think of boys' names. Boys' names seemed to fit better.

> I can't believe it. I even changed the sex of the bees in my story from female to male deliberately.

> I could have just as easily had a girl at the centre of my story. I don't know why I didn't. (Gilbert, 1985, p. 19)

What had come to seem 'natural' and 'right' for these students was what passes as the dominant tradition in children's literature: it seemed 'natural' to write about boys, 'natural' to have boys as the active protagonists of the narratives, 'natural' to use the male pronoun and male names. While 82 per cent of these students were female, only 25 per cent of the stories featured females as chief characters. It had also become natural for these female students to write from a male perspective.

The naturalisation of generic conventions is a major difficulty in the classroom because it obscures the discursive and therefore ideological construction of particular genres. While, for instance, stories featuring animal characters vary a great deal in their styles and purposes, one of the striking features of such stories is the ubiquitous use of the male pronoun. Many popular and favourite picture story books consistently use the male pronoun, even when it would make no difference to narrative credibility to have used female pronouns. Almost without exception children's animal stories feature female animals when a stereotypical female role is required, as when a mother/nurturer is needed or someone is lost (see Gilbert, 1989a).

Similarly the folk and fairy tales commonly used in contemporary classrooms are immediately recognisable and familiar because of their gendered conventions. Such tales rely upon resolution devices like the 'happy-ever-after' marriage, or a tragic death for a forsaken lover, and adopt clear stereotypes for heroines. Danger lurks for maidens without men or families; women are clearly not meant to be able to exist alone. And the generic formulas do not alter significantly with other reading material commonly available in schools, or with popular television texts. As we saw in chapters 3 and 4, television soaps and the teen romance formula novels rely upon gendered stereotypes to function and consequently be 'read'. So do most of the popular children's and young adults' fiction forms: the sexuality novels of Judy Blume, the 'problem' novels from Maureen Stewart, the bizarre fantasies of Roald Dahl. When students try to write, they cannot write beyond the genre forms—or the generic play—they know as possible: they are locked into their own (often limited) intertextuality. Playing with various genre forms is possible, but it takes an extremely confident student to 'play', and an astute and perceptive teacher to recognise such 'play'. The familiar—the conventional, the recognisable—is always safe: safe for students, safe for teachers, and therefore safe for assessment.

However, students do 'play' with various generic conventions, and sometimes a recognition of such play indicates how confining and restricting are the conventions of popular fiction. Consider, for example, the following story, *Italia*.

ITALIA

Author's note: Hi! My name is Helen and I'd like to tell you about 'Italia'. Visiting Italy is not always the glamorous country for tourists. This is a story about a wild goose chase in the Italian environment.

Chapter 1: Starting my Trip
I decided to visit Italy for a holiday but I didn't know that I would have to come back to get a rest from my everlasting long and tiring holiday.

I arrived in Rome at 1.00 pm, on the 16th October, awaiting for the Triboni family to take me into their home and enjoy the loving hospitality of their farm. I was 24 and Linda, one of their children, was 25. Linda and I went to school with each other in Australia fifteen years earlier.

After a long wait, I recognized a face in the oncoming crowd. She had long black hair which curled around her face. Suddenly she started yelling, 'Catherine! Catherine!' At the sound of her voice I knew it was Linda.

'Linda! Linda! I'm over here.'

Linda immediately turned her head in my direction sensing that I was near. Linda rushed over, 'Oh Catherine, I'm so glad to see you.'

'And I'm glad to be here.'

We said this in the most dramatic way possible.

I arrived on the Triboni's farm half an hour later. The Tribonis were nice people and all of them acted as my own family.

Milan: The next day I left for Venice where all the action was to start. I arrived in Milan, speeding absolutely, forgetting where I was.

A cop saw me and pulled me up for speeding. As soon as he pulled me up I realized he was a fake but as politely as he could he said, 'Briongiorno.' I had been studying Italian for four years and understood that he was saying 'good-morning'.

'Chow,' I answered back. He could see I was Australian and spoke in English.

'Now listen little Miss. I'll let you off this time but be on your way.' I got into my BMW which had been transported over, and drove away not knowing why he had been so kind.

Chapter 2: A Familiar Face
It was an hour after the speeding incident when I noticed another policeman standing beside the road, in fact he looked quite similar to the one I had met earlier. He held out his hand to say 'Stop!' and then motioned me over. As I got closer I realized it was the same policeman and again he spoke to me in his harsh words. 'You're off the hook this time,' he told me in a completely different voice, 'but be on your way and remember speeding is against the law.'

I left in a hurry for I knew his temper would shoot at me if I stayed any longer. I was half an hour down the road when I saw in my rearvision mirror the cop pull out behind me.

'Something fishy going on here,' I said to myself.

Chapter 3: A Third Incident
'He must think I'm really dumb if he thinks I can't see him.'

Then he disappeared around a corner. I saw a roadside cafeteria and decided I needed some lunch. I was sitting peacefully when the young policeman walked into the cafe. Suddenly I raced out of the cafeteria with wallet in one hand and lunch in the other. He gave me a stern look as I drove out of the parking lot and to my friend's home.

'Are you ready?' I called when I got there.

'Yeah! Just let me put my things in your car,' Emma yelled back. Emma was coming with me on my journey and returning to Australia where she formerly came from.

Chapter 4: Quatroi

Emma and I left for Pisa straight away. We arrived and decided that the Leaning Tower of Pisa would be our first tour. Emma and I both had slippery shoes and were almost going to slide off the building when a hand grabbed our arms. When we saw the policeman's face we were about to run when he caught us and took us to some sort of hideout. There he kept an eye on our every move day in, day out for three days. We slept on hard straw beds behind steel bars and had very little conversation. Then he let us go on a good behaviour bond.

'What a strange man!' said Emma with a dazzled brain.

'He's been bugging me for quite a number of days,' I replied, 'and he looks to be a fake,' I said, now a little puzzled myself.

We travelled for seven days without any trouble, through Naples and Sardinia then quite surprisingly, we met the same man at the airport when boarding the aeroplane.

Chapter 5: The Explanation

We arrived in our well known Australian environment tired and a little sick. Our holiday had been busy and definitely not what we had expected.

We walked in to meet my fiancee, my mother-in-law to be, my own mother and father talking to the stranger who had been bugging us for ten days.

'And what do we have to say about this,' said Emma, talking to herself.

My fiancee overheard and answered her question. 'Well,your mother, my mother, and myself decided we wanted to keep a check on you and your friend, so Mike here, dressed up as a cop and followed you for a time. Finally he lost track but caught up at Pisa and caught you so he could keep a thorough check on you.'

'Well, I suppose it was all in a good cause although it did make our holiday very confusing,' I said firmly. And that was all to be said about our holiday and eventually all was forgotten.

Italia was written by a ten-year-old middle-class girl in a provincial Australian primary school. The interesting thing about this story is that while the girl has drawn rather obviously from a predictable generic formula, she seems to have had some difficulty constructing a story from within the frameworks possible. Her text exhibits a number of tensions and unresolved conflicts. The female subject position she tries to create is not completely clear, largely because the female position traditionally constructed through romantic ideology is one of female passivity and dependence, and yet the subject position sought for this story's protagonist is one of activity and independence.

The story is, we are told, about 'a wild goose chase in the Italian environment'. A young Australian woman sets out on a touring trip of Italy—complete with her imported BMW—but is constantly harassed by a man disguised as a policeman. After being captured and imprisoned by the man, she is eventually freed and allowed to continue her trip. On her return to Australia she discovers that the man who had imprisoned her was a friend of her fiancé's who had been sent to Italy, by her fiancé and her parents, to spy and 'keep a check' on her.

The story could be unravelled in a number of ways, but it rather obviously demonstrates the limitations of the subject position constructed through romantic ideology. When this young writer tries to write about adventure, she ends up being tied to marriage, fidelity, and female dependence on male protection. When she tries to write about independent travel, she instead writes about male erosion of that freedom. When she tries to write about a woman on her own, she writes about a daughter and a fiancé. This ten-year-old writer has resisted the female subject position constructed by romance discourses, but she seems to know of no other. She has fallen back upon the comfortable, almost 'natural' seeming formulaic pattern of girl reunited with Mr Right—a pattern that is repeated in a number of other discourses through a number of other signifying practices that this girl will be familiar with. But her text shows the uneasy and incomplete acceptance of such subjectivity as her story threatens to run away from its generic conventions.

The way this girl writer is trapped within traditional generic frames, and their clearly gendered conventions, has limited her opportunity to construct a story which lies outside such gendered differentiation. And yet she has tried. She has resisted the inevitability of marriage, physical domination, and restricted freedom. But she has no speaking position of authority available to her, no alternative discourses which offer her other ways of constructing gendered subjects. She does not yet know how to write 'as a woman'—or at least a woman constructed and positioned by discourses other than romantic ideology.

Writing (and reading) as a man

In chapter 2 we quoted the Australian author, Thea Astley, describing the decision she had made to write 'as a man': ' "It's a woman's book" they'd say, as if there was something wrong with that. So when I was eighteen or nineteen I thought to myself that the only way one could have any sort of validity was to write as a male...' (in Baker, 1986: p. 42). We suspect that this decision is also made—unconsciously in most cases—by many girls in classrooms as an inevitable response to their recognition that women's ideas, women's experiences, women's speech, women's stories, women's television shows, women's magazines, women's music, women's art forms are deemed to be of lesser value than are men's. As we argued in chapter 4, most girls quickly learn how devalued are many of the language forms traditionally associated with women.

It could also be argued that there are seldom discourses of power available to women which position them as speaking subjects. Most school discourses position woman as the spoken subject—as the passive, marginalised 'other' (Baker and Davies, 1989)—with noticeable consequences for classroom language interaction. In Adrienne Rich's words: '... listen to a woman groping for language in which to express what is on her mind, sensing that the terms of academic discourse are not her language, trying to cut down her thoughts to the dimensions of a discourse not intended for her...' (Rich, 1980: p. 243). The subject matter girls are likely to choose when they select writing topics, and the reading positions they often take up in relation to set school texts, are clear indicators of this discursive marginalisation of women. As example, consider these typical yet disturbing results from one very small survey of girls' and boys' responses to a specific writing topic.

When asked by their female teachers to write about the person they most admired, sixteen-year-old male and female students in this survey chose predominantly from a male field. In a single-sex class of 25 boys, only four boys wrote about women: three wrote about their mothers, and one about 'females' in general. The 21 men they chose as their most admired characters were all contemporary figures. They included politicians (e.g., Ronald Reagan, Bob Hawke); movie and pop stars (e.g., Mel Gibson, Prince, George Michael); sportsmen (e.g., Wally Lewis, racing car drivers); and their fathers. By comparison, in a single-sex girls' class of thirteen, only five chose to write of women they admired. They selected a hairdresser, a friend, Marilyn Monroe, Mother Theresa, and the Aboriginal poet Kath Walker. The eight men they admired included historical figures like Albert Einstein and Leonardo da Vinci, but also current media and sports stars like Paul Hogan and Alan Langer.

Few teachers would be surprised by this selection the girls had made, particularly given the paucity of information generally made available to sixteen-year-olds about women they might admire, alive or dead, or about the way in which societies recognise and choose people to admire. And many teachers often unthinkingly perpetuate this male focus by prescribing writing and reading tasks which do assume that young women will be more interested in men and a male perspective (Frith, 1981). One has only to look at the novels, plays and poetry still set for particular study in secondary schools and university departments, to realise that *women's* literature—particularly women's literature that directly addresses issues concerned with the experience of being a woman— is in a minority on such courses (Lake, 1988; Carlson, 1989).

And yet if students are to interpret the texts in the traditional (conventional) sense, they will need to take up the dominant reading position, even when such reading positions are often, as feminist aesthetics has indicated, misogynistic positions. Women read about women as the 'other'—viewing themselves through the male gaze. Little wonder that adolescent girls often choose to write from a male persona (Gilbert, 1983); it may be the only persona whose textual construction seems *known* and *natural*. The gendered reality of the classroom may also make it difficult for a teacher to work with women's perspectives—to move away from the dominant male speaking position—as Baker and Davies report in their work on classroom interaction (1989), and as Judith Williamson (1981/2) noted in a lesson dealing with sexual stereotypes.

Writing against the grain: resistance and rewriting

However, if writing pedagogy can be wrenched away from its personalist roots, and grounded more securely in a framework which acknowledges discursive power networks and the textual practices which maintain such networks, possibilities exist for deconstructing written texts in the classroom, and reconstructing alternative texts. While it is not possible to stand outside of discourse, it is possible to recognise the discursive frameworks that surround us, and critically to consider the production of certain generic conventions and expectations that serve to maintain those frameworks.

'Play' is then possible, through the reversal and rejection of conventions, and the construction of texts that parody and reconstruct. 'Play' becomes more powerful, however, and more useful to young women, if the conventions that are being played with are linked to their discursive power bases, and to broader semiotic systems constructing gendered identities. It is one thing, for instance, to parody a *Dolly Fiction* story. It is quite another to understand how the conventions of such formula fiction serve to perpetuate romance ideology, and how such ideology constructs particular gendered subject positions. While classrooms often work with parody, seldom are the parodic inventions themselves deconstructed and discursively located.

Consider, for instance, the following story, *The Intelligent Princess*, written by another ten-year-old middle-class girl.

THE INTELLIGENT PRINCESS

Chapter 1: Bored

Zillah was bored. It was another silly day. The king tried on his new robes while making sure they were 100% pure gold, and her mother was hiring more and more servants and also trying to count her money. None of the servants, royal relations, or the royal majesties themselves took any notice of the princess upstairs who was supposed to be engrossed in listening to *Wham* but was actually falling asleep listening to *Careless Whispers* for the 55th time.

'Why don't you marry a nice wealthy man and have a happy life?' her mother used to say.

'Poohie, I don't want to,' she'd say back. 'Haven't you any taste, mum?'

One morning, Zillah walked downstairs and her mum and dad were talking seriously about her marrying.

'Ahem!' she attracted their attention. They turned their heads her way.

'OK. I'll go out and seek a handsome prince if you really want me to. I'll be back in about a week,' she said and slunk off.

Her mother supplied the food and her father the travelling goods. She set out.

Chapter 2: Bags of Candy

Not far away from her home town there was a gloomy old castle called Mitredom. Mitredom had a gloomy reputation because of its gloomy occupants. The gloomiest of all was the prince of Mitredom himself. All he did was stare out the window all day. Whenever someone miserable walked past his door, he'd get even gloomier still. However when a very attractive girl adorned with diamonds walked up the path to his door, he lost all his gloom and ran down to meet her.

'Will you marry me?' were the first words that came out of him. 'I'll give you 800,000,000 bags of candy!'

'Candy? Piffle. Candy? Pooh. An intelligent princess won't do for you!' she said boldly, and stomped off.

Chapter 3: The Prince Misses Out
Soon Zillah stopped at a glistening lake. On a sign leaning against the trunk of a willow was a sign: **Greenwood Lake: Green Glass Castle This Way**.

Lunch? She sat down on a grassy patch and got out a tuna fish sandwich with a glass of lemonade and enjoyed it. She had sneaked her new *Dire Straits* tape and tape-recorder from the castle, along with a short red silk mini skirt, black fish net stockings, a red velvet sleeveless t-shirt, and dangling ear-rings. She put everything together and even popped some bubblegum into her mouth and chewed and danced happily. Soon she sensed that someone was watching her. She stopped the music and looked around. She couldn't see anything. Then she heard a rustle in the bushes. Out stepped a handsome prince. He came up to her and said, 'Busy tonight?' Zillah blew a bubble in his face and chanted, 'Roses are red, emeralds are green. My face is funny, but yours is a scream. Thank you for letting me have the pleasure of saying that, 'she said, and packed up all ready to head on.

'What a drag. I was having fun,' she thought.

Chapter 4: One Shot
Soon Zillah arrived at Green Glass Castle. She put down her bags and knocked on the glass lion knocker. A handsome tanned prince opened the door and ushered her inside to sit by a gold framed jade table with two glasses of lemonade sitting ready on top of it. The prince waited for her to sit down and when she did said in a definite manner, 'I've been expecting you. In the Star Guide for the Royalty Magazine it said: *Your future companion shall meet you this week.* These glasses of lemonade have been ready and waiting. I had a couple of false alarms, but this one can't be. What's your business, companion?' he asked.

'I'm looking for a husband, actually,' she said 'I don't want to, but my parents insisted.'

'I see,' he said with a crafty look.

'And you?'

'Oh, I'm a suntanner,' he said proudly.

'What is your name?' Zillah asked.

'Glen Roe.'

She frowned with disgust.

'Yes, isn't it horrible? he said embarrassedly.

'Mine is Zillah, Jane, Heather, Sapphira Antoinette,' she said. 'My grandmother was Marie Antoinette. I've got her head in my room for a souvenir. She's frowning.'

Chapter 5: Servants
Zillah and Glen agreed to set out together on Zillah's quest. Soon they came to the crystal palace, which was one hundred years old. They stopped at the huge iron gates which were standing open, and bowed down to the guards.

'May we see the prince, please?' Zillah asked quite timidly and innocently. The two guards exchanged glances and started to laugh hysterically. Zillah and Glen walked straight through the gates and left the two guards to themselves. They walked down a corridor and into a little room. There, sitting on a velvet cushion, was a little sullen boy. He brightened up as soon as he saw them and shouted, 'Are you my new servants?'

'Well—uh—ah—yeah!' they said.

Chapter 6: Departure
It was not long before they were all good friends. Zillah made croissants for the little boy, while Glen sewed him a velvet cushion made of silk and crusted with diamonds and emeralds.

One night they were all sitting at the fire when Zillah remembered her parents.

'What a drag. I promised them I'd be back by tomorrow, but I don't want to leave,' she said.

'Hey—I would like to see your rubies—they're my birthstones, you know,' the little prince piped in.

Zillah laughed. 'Start packing!'

This is rather obviously a modernised and rather liberated fairy tale, and, not surprisingly, this particular writer had encountered a range of textual material of that kind. However, this is not common. While feminist versions of fairy and folk tales are one of the few forms of alternative texts available to young women, as Bronwyn Davies records in her work (1989), such tales are not always read through counter-sexist frames: children are not always discursively positioned to accept such versions of gender identity. Such stories are also not commonly available in school libraries and in classrooms. Yet, as Davies argues, and as the *The Intelligent Princess* partially demonstrates, 'feminist stories are an invaluable resource for the imaginative construction of subject positionings outside of traditional gendered relations' (p. 46).

In this particular story it is a princess—rather than a prince—who is on a quest, and it is the princess's adventures which form the narrative. The quest is to find a husband, albeit against the Princess's will. Her parents have insisted that she find a marriage partner. Perhaps this writer could not conceive of any other goal that would drive a young woman on a search? Her general textual background of traditional literature would probably have been of little help here. While warrior kings and princes can go in search of dragons, wizards, treasure, or the Holy Grail, queens and princesses have been preoccupied with keeping themselves beautiful, arranging for the elimination of sexual rivals, or waiting for their husbands/brothers/fathers to return from their quests.

The intelligent princess in this story has two encounters with men on her journey, and both are unwanted male intrusions which seek to limit the princess's freedom. For example, the prince of Mitredom runs out of his castle to meet her: '"Will you marry me?" were the first words that came out of him. "I'll give you 800 000 000 bags of candy!"' The intelligent princess naturally refuses such an offer: '"Candy? Piffle. Candy? Pooh. An intelligent princess won't do for you!" she said boldly, and stomped off.' However, at her next stop— Greenwood Lake—she relaxes with her packed lunch and tape recorder only to hear a rustle in the bushes. A handsome prince has been spying on her. He invites her out for the evening, but she rejects him, packs up and heads off again: '"What a drag. I was having fun," she thought'. The princess moves on to Green Glass Castle, where she meets a third young man, another prince. This prince calls her 'companion', and asks her her business. The conversation exchange between the two is noticeable for the apparent equality of power of the two speakers, and for the princess's forthrightness. The young prince decides to join the princess on her quest. At their first stop they meet a young child (also a prince), befriend him, and finally all return to the princess's home. A potential union between the prince and the princess is unspoken but implied.

This story is rich in its resistance to a number of conventions. The princess is forthright to her parents and the princes, she is independent and unafraid to travel alone, and she is astute and assertive in her dealings with men. But the story is also an indication of how confined this girl's narrative has been by the textual patterns she knew, and by her understanding of what it means to be a woman. A princess's quest is likely to be one involving marriage; intruders on female independence and privacy are likely to be men wanting to dominate and control women; women, as objects, are constantly watched and observed.

The last section of the narrative introduces some interesting alternatives that this young girl would like for her quest. The princess and her companion meet a sullen little boy prince who mistakes them at first for his new servants. In this girl's narrative world, have the male and the female to be reduced to the same position of powerlessness as servants before they can fully be equal? The sullen young boy eventually leaves home to live with the princess, but not before the prince and princess have lived with him in an ungendered domestic environment: the prince sews, and the princess cooks. The young boy then becomes almost the child of this new union: there need be no sexual interference to the princess, no pregnancy, no childbirth. The girl child can fulfil her female expectations to marry and produce children yet remain a girl child.

After having read children's stories in ways like this, the need to provide alternative stories to students, so that signs of resistance to passive female subject positions might be fostered rather than ignored, becomes more apparent. Once the stability and apparent permanence of a story are disrupted, then the conventions that have held it together can be unpacked, re-read, and then rewritten. As we indicated in chapters 3 and 4, popular cultural texts offer many opportunities for work of this type. When the generic conventions of television texts and formula novels are unravelled and discursively traced, then reading and writing become activities through which gendered bipolarity becomes visible, recognisable, 'read'. It is then possible to write against the grain, to take up other speaking positions.

Writing against the grain is thus about writing against conventions that construct women in ways that are demeaning and restricting. It is about learning to write against the predictable patterns of popular cultural texts, because such texts almost uniformly fashion the female subject in ways that serve the patriarchal gender order. The main difficulty associated with writing in this way is that students—and their teachers—are usually inadequately textually prepared for such tasks. Reading against the grain is as difficult as writing against the grain, for it demands that readers resist the seductive coherence of the familiar and comfortable. But without such reading practices, writing 'against the grain' cannot occur, and if there is to be any potential in the writing classroom for young women, it must lie in a critical consideration of the nature and purpose of written texts, and their discursive location.

Part III

Rewriting the texts

6

Feminist classroom practice: possibilities for challenge and change

Revision—the act of looking back, of seeing with fresh eyes, of entering an old text from a new critical direction—is for women more than a chapter in cultural history: it is an act of survival. Until we can understand the assumptions in which we are drenched we cannot know ourselves. (Rich, 1980, quoted in Oakley, 1984: p. 2)

In the first chapter of this book we wrote: 'The basic starting point for our work is that while schooling is an important site for the reproduction of gender relations, it is also a site for intervention and change'. Since then we have explored the roles played by various cultural texts in the construction of femininity and have also considered to some extent how these texts are used in the classroom. In this chapter we turn to a consideration of the specific discussions in Part II for the development of a feminist classroom practice, and explore the possibilities for radical change through the cultural politics of the classroom.

We have particularly focussed on the cultural sphere in the book: on the transmission and circulation of *meanings* about gender by various cultural texts and on their role in the construction of femininity. While it is clear that gender ideologies are not passively internalised, those mediated through schooling, along with those circulated in other arenas, become part of a repertoire of ways of thinking about what it means to 'be female'. Consequently, we have argued that it is this range of available discourses which is crucial in providing the framework within which the construction of femininity takes place.

The analyses in Part II show that, despite the possibility of oppositional readings, popular cultural texts tend to legitimate patriarchal gender relations. Although it is clear that such cultural texts relate in complex ways to girls' everyday lives, girls' experiences and subjectivities are always already structured by patriarchal gender relations and often oppositional readings will merely be a diversion, a way of coping, and not lead to any real change in gender relations. Furthermore, it seems that popular cultural texts legitimate gender relations as much by the way they enter into the politics of girls' and women's everyday lives as through the ideological messages they transmit.

In the case of soap opera viewing, we find that teenage girls already show well established feminine patterns in the way they use television in their lives, both in terms of viewing patterns and in the way in which the programmes are used to rehearse problems and contradictions in their own lives. The appeal of soap operas for this group lies in the focus of the genre on feelings and relationships, and in the opportunities they offer for 'time out' from the 'real world'. In chapter 3 we discussed the view that soap operas offer the potential for oppositional and resistive readings because they tend to play with the myths of patriarchy and allow them to be questioned by their audiences. For example, in soaps the perfect, happy, stable family is an ideal which is never achieved. However, despite these apparently progressive possibilities offered by soap opera texts, we concluded that teenage girls' limited life experiences would make them less likely to make oppositional readings than older women viewers. We also concluded that given the concerns teenage girls express about their futures, it would seem unlikely that the contradictions offered by soaps would be very helpful to them. Oppositional readings are likely to be 'lost' among the dominant versions of femininity constructed not only directly through the television texts, but also through the plethora of advertising texts that accompany—and complete—the viewing of soaps. Consequently, we concluded that the gendered subjectivity posited by the soaps was limited, stereotypical, and unlikely to challenge the patriarchal gender order. The discourses of soap operas may be relatively progressive in that they play with the myths of patriarchy, but that does not mean that alternative discourses could not be more empowering, particularly for teenage girls and young women.

In chapter 4 we suggested that romance novels appear to offer some resolution to the 'problem' of becoming feminine, by presenting a possible solution to some of the contradictions in teenage girls' lives. And we argued that despite some claims that the 'escape' which romance reading offers has progressive elements, the discourse of romance is a patriarchal discourse which locks women into passivity and dependency. The evidence presented in chapter 5 shows that girls' writing reflects the narrow range of discourses about gender which is available to them and shows the difficulties they encounter in writing 'against the grain', that is, in writing outside of patriarchal conventions.

However, we have already indicated that we regard schools and classrooms as important sites for intervention in the construction of femininity and we need to carefully think through the implications of the case studies we have presented. In developing approaches for the classroom we need to ask, firstly, what is the significance of popular cultural texts in girls' lives and how do we take account of this in the curriculum? And secondly, how do we use popular cultural texts in the classroom to challenge traditional versions of femininity and develop new and alternative versions? In other words, what possibilities are there for 'fashioning the feminine' in new ways?

The remaining part of this chapter will address these questions. In the next section we consider general issues relating to policies on the education of girls which are relevant to our more specific focus, and then we follow this by a consideration of the way in which feminist pedagogy is related to subjectivity and change. The last section of the chapter focusses upon alternative ways to fashion the feminine, by describing approaches offered through cultural studies, and through alternative textual practices.

The curriculum and change

In Australia in recent years there has been a growing concern with the education of girls at the policy level, and various aspects of schooling have been targeted for reform. The development of *The National Policy on the Education of Girls in Australian Schools* (Schools Commission, 1987) has been an encouraging sign of change, although how much real progress has been made in addressing the education of girls is questionable. Lyn Yates has suggested that much of the apparent attention to gender issues is illusory and that:

> with very few exceptions, when policies have been framed for all students, they have still been insensitive to gender and sexism, to issues concerning girls and women as a category. They have been insensitive either by ignoring this area, or by assuming that the mention of terms like 'inclusive' or 'non-sexist' disposes of the problem when it is really given no force in the policy in question (1988: p. 41)

Furthermore, the context of 'economic rationalism' which has influenced educational policy development in recent years has tended to work against any trends to improve the position of women in education and employment. The result is that while the position of women and girls is on the official educational policy agenda at last, that position is extremely precarious given the current economic and political context (Henry and Taylor, 1989).

One focus for change in policy documents has been the traditional school curriculum which, as we have discussed, fails to reflect the experiences and contribution of women in history and in contemporary society. Consequently, the notion of the 'gender-inclusive curriculum' was developed in the early 1980s and has become influential in feminist work in education. It has also been adopted and used in some official policy documents at both federal and state levels (see, for example, Schools Commission, 1984). What a gender-inclusive curriculum might mean, and how such a curriculum might be used in a way that is genuinely empowering for girls and young women, needs to be clarified. Some approaches to the 'inclusive curriculum' attempt to take account of class and ethnicity as well as gender, to cater for 'all students'. The result is often that gender issues are marginalised. Although there is a need to take account of the way in which class, gender and ethnicity *interact* in shaping particular individuals, it is also necessary to consider these issues *separately* when curriculum and pedagogy are being developed (Yates, 1988). Different approaches are likely to be needed to effectively address each of these issues, and there are potential conflicts in trying to deal with them together, as is documented in some of Weiler's (1988) accounts of the experiences of feminist teachers.

Many of the policies and curriculum approaches which have developed over the last decade take insufficient account of the complexities involved in the construction of femininity. As we argued in chapter 1 of this book, an understanding of the cultural perspectives of teenage girls is crucial if feminist educators are to work appropriately with them. Too often, teenage girls' concerns, particularly their interest in romance, have not been taken seriously and have been brushed aside as unimportant. Alternative approaches have failed to begin with life experiences, and here it is important to recognise that these will vary with class and ethnic differences. Often it has been assumed that all that is necessary is to provide 'alternative models' for girls, with the result that teenage girls and young women, particularly those from working-class backgrounds, have become alienated from feminists and feminism. In our concern to encourage 'awareness' we have been guilty of imposing our own 'regulatory mechanism' (feminism) to replace romantic ideology. An understanding of the complexities of the construction of femininity shows why such approaches are unlikely to be successful. We will discuss the problems with such an approach in more detail later in this chapter.

The challenge for feminist educators is to work *with* girls and young women and help them to reflect critically on their own lives and futures. As Judith Williamson (1981/2) has argued, we cannot *teach* ideologies—or even *teach about* ideologies. We can only try to bring students to an understanding, from their own experiences, of the way that we are all caught up in ideological processes in our everyday lives. Unless students can make sense of the issues in terms of their own lives and experiences they are likely to become alienated or resistant, and educational programmes will be counter-productive.

It is important that teachers and others working with girls and young women are aware of the conflicts and concerns which this group express, and that girls are encouraged to explore and to discuss with one another the contradictions and pressures they face. These concerns, as we discussed in chapter 1, centre on girls' futures (both in the workforce and as mothers), on sexuality, and on issues related to age and maturity. They should not be dismissed as unimportant and irrelevant because of an educational preoccupation with career planning.

One implication of the conflicts relating to sexuality is that care is needed in dealing with any expressions of sexuality by teenage girls at school, given that many of them are in fact sexually mature young women. Teachers should avoid perpetuating the labelling practices of the 'politics of reputation' in the comments they make to students (see chapter 1), and should rather encourage girls' own resistance to the labels imposed on them. In relation to the femininity/adolescence conflict, it is also important to encourage resistance and independence, rather than constantly to pressure girls to be 'mature' and 'feminine'.

It would also seem to be wise to foster collectivity in girls and young women. McRobbie (1980) has suggested that if girls were more involved with all-girl sub-cultures, rather than early involvement with a steady boyfriend, they might gain some much needed collective confidence. One way of encouraging collectivity is through provision of single-sex facilities and programmes for girls. Certainly many activities involving critical reflection need to be organised in all-girl groups and also need to be based on co-operative work.

It is important to take account of girls' and young women's concerns about their futures as childrearers and to address these concerns in the curriculum. Blackburn (1982) has advocated studies of women's experience of parenting in relation to working life and such studies can be a focus for the critical discussion of girls' future lives. This could be done through a work education programme—to be developed as a central part of the curriculum and integrated with other subject areas. Such a work education programme could involve a general study of work in society, including historical aspects such as the effects of the Industrial Revolution and the impact of technological change on women's work, as well as discussion about childbearing/childrearing, and combining paid work and parenting. It could also include more traditional 'career education' components such as information about a wide range of jobs, work experience and decision-making skills.

The report *Girls and Tomorrow* concluded as follows: 'Schools are not providing girls with the necessary information and skills on which to base decisions about their post-school life...' (Schools Commission, 1984: p. 31). Consequently, it would seem that a work education programme also needs to include demographic information about changes in society relating to women's employment patterns, marriage and family size, family breakdown and the feminisation of poverty. Associated projects such as the investigation of availability and needs for childcare in a community could be valuable. Decision making and life planning need also to be encouraged, but in the context of information about social trends in Australian society previously mentioned. Documented programmes which take account of some of these aspects include 'Future Studies' (described in Ballenden, 1984), 'Women and Work' (in Ballenden et al., 1984) and 'Women in the Workforce and Change' (in Foster, 1984).

Subjectivity and change

Throughout the book we have highlighted the complexities of the construction of femininity and have shown that the power of gender ideologies lies in the fact that they work at an unconscious level, through the structuring of desires, as well as at a conscious or rational level. In chapter 1 we argued that the construction of a gendered subjectivity was crucial to the reproduction of patriarchal gender relations, and in chapter 2 we showed the roles played by both language processes and pedagogical processes in this reproduction. We have accepted the argument that subjectivity is not necessarily acquired in any unified or coherent way. It is struggled over and imperfectly held because different discourses offer different subject positions or points of view, many of which are contradictory and incompatible. We also argued that the acceptance of a particular subject position inevitably means the acceptance of a gendered subjectivity: 'Everything we do signifies compliance or resistance to dominant norms of what it means to be a woman' (Weedon, 1987: pp. 86–7).

We have already referred to Judith Williamson's comments about the difficulties of helping students move to an awareness of ideology. She has argued that although it is essential to begin with students' experiences, this is in fact problematic. It is personally threatening for many students to place their lives under scrutiny as their very sense of themselves is at stake (1981/2, 1985). Drawing on her experiences of teaching media studies to 'tech. school' students in Britain, Williamson comments: 'If we mean what we write about the formation of the subject through social discourses, and so on, and then direct the thrust of our teaching *at* social discourse, we ought to *know* that we are thereby hacking at the very roots of those formed subjects' (1981/2: p. 85). And, in relation to her own experience, Williamson discusses how traumatic it can be to first 'see' that social reality is ideological. The other important insight she offers is that students learn about ideologies when they actually have to confront them in a practical situation. In Williamson's view, students can never understand these issues purely intellectually; they need to bump up against ideologies in the course of practical, productive work (1981/2). For these reasons fashioning the feminine in new ways will be difficult and challenging, because it will involve deconstructing dominant ideologies and changing subjectivities.

Furthermore, fashioning the feminine in new ways is even more difficult because of what Rosalind Coward (1984) calls the 'lure of pleasure'. Various definitions of female desire are offered to women in their everyday lives—through 'feminine pleasures' such as cooking, fashion, soap operas and romantic fiction—and these work to sustain the patriarchal gender order through the production of female pleasure and desire: '...our subjectivity and identity are formed in the definitions of desire which encircle us. These are the experiences which make change such a difficult and daunting task, for female desire is constantly lured by discourses which sustain male privilege' (1984: p. 16). However, in her essays on *Female Desire*, Coward attempts to highlight the possibilities for the development of alternative definitions of femininity, through addressing the contradictions, gaps and precariousness of the existing definitions (1984).

Critical educational theory

Critical educational theory may well help to extend these understandings of the construction of subjectivity and the possibilities for change by identifying spaces for opposition and resistance within educational discourses. A number of feminist educators, to whom we will refer in the following section, have found aspects of such work relevant to the development of feminist pedagogies, even though, in general, male critical theorists have given little attention to gender issues.

Henry Giroux's work does not directly deal with gender relations, but his approach to the concept of ideology is useful in theorising the links between gender relations and subjectivity, and also in thinking about change:

> As both the medium and the outcome of lived experience, ideology functions not only to limit human action but also to enable it...Central to understanding how ideology functions in the interest of social reproduction is the issue of how ideology works on and through individuals to secure their basic consent to the basic ethos and practices of the dominant society. Equally important for an understanding of how ideology functions in the interest of social transformation is the issue of

how ideology creates the terrain for self-reflection and transformative action (1984: p. 314)

Following Gramsci, Giroux discusses the three specific levels which are involved in the interface between ideology and individual experience: 'the sphere of the unconscious and the structure of needs; the realm of common sense; and the sphere of critical consciousness' (1984: p. 315), and also examines how the relations between ideology and each of these spheres of meaning and practice are involved in both social reproduction and transformation.

Giroux emphasises the extent to which historical and societal forces are implicated in the structuring of individual experience at each of the three levels, including the production of needs and desires. He argues that once the extent to which subjectivity is historically and socially structured is acknowledged, the groundwork is set 'for a critical encounter between oneself and the dominant society' (1984: p. 318). This occurs through ideology critique: the analysis of everyday taken-for-granted common-sense practices, which, instead of being treated as 'given', 'must be viewed within historical and social relations that are produced and socially constructed' (1984: p. 322). Giroux also discusses the importance of ideology critique in relation to cultural 'texts' such as films and books, and advocates the use of critique to go beyond deconstruction of the texts to a reconstruction which serves radical needs. However, it is the critical consciousness, which 'lays bare the historically and socially sedimented values at work in the construction of knowledge, social relations and material practices' (1984: p. 323) which Giroux views as crucial in transformation and change. In later explorations of these issues, using the work of Mikhail Bakhtin (1981), Giroux gives language and discourse a central emphasis as 'technologies of power' in theorising the construction of experience and subjectivity (1986).

The Brazilian educator Paulo Freire has also been influential in the development of radical curriculum approaches which are concerned with transforming social relations (1972, 1985). Freire's notion of empowerment through 'conscientisation'— critical reflection on the circumstances of lived experiences together with action—has relevance here. Freire, too, is interested in how social forces shape subjectivity and how these processes can be challenged. Ira Shor (1987) has used these strategies with college students in the USA and writes of the importance of helping students to 'extraordinarily re-experience the ordinary'. He makes the important point that, though his critical pedagogy is situated in the themes and experiences of the students, the aim is not merely to 'exploit or endorse the given but seeks to transcend it...We gain a distance from the given by abstracting it from its unfamiliar surroundings and studying it in unfamiliar ways, until our perceptions of it and society are challenged' (Shor, in Freire and Shor, 1987: p. 104).

Cultural politics and change

Recent work on critical pedagogy emphasises the importance of cultural politics and places education in its wider cultural context. For example, in the collection of articles entitled *Critical Pedagogy and Cultural Power* (Livingstone, 1987), there is 'an attempt to understand how forms of subjectivity are regulated and transformed through the structured character of such social forms as language, ideologies, myths, significations, and narratives, (p. xv). Cultural politics are seen as an important arena for radical change, both in relation to socialism (see, for example, Lingard and Symes, 1985) and in relation to socialist feminism (Kaplan, 1986). In this context, Williamson's insights about the use of media studies as a way of connecting issues of personal identity with cultural activity have been significant, and she views such activity as politically important: 'It is only as familiar structures of meaning are shaken and taken apart that new ones can form. And looking at things differently makes it possible to act differently' (Williamson, 1989: p. 6). For instance, the introductory statement to a recent anthology of Australian women's poetry attempts to place women's writing in the realm of cultural politics, by discussing the importance of rethinking the world in order to reconstruct the world. In a perceptive discussion of the stages in the evolution of a feminist consciousness, Susan Hampton and Kate Llewellyn claim that after the awareness of oppression and the radical questioning of social structures, there follows a stage of creation: '[m]aking something new is to imagine different grids on reality, other views on the world' (Hampton and Llewellyn, 1986: p. 5).

Towards a feminist critical pedagogy

While aspects of critical educational theory can be utilised in the construction of a feminist pedagogy, Patti Lather has argued that the critical theorists have failed to recognise that women's studies is, in fact, an example of what they themselves are attempting to develop: transformative practice. Lather describes women's studies as 'intellectual consciousness raising', which she suggests can be conceptualised as counter-hegemonic work. Consequently, she argues that critical theory and women's studies 'would each benefit from an attempt to explore the "practical political activity" that is women's studies' (1984: p. 30).

Many feminists have used 'consciousness raising' as an important approach in teaching (Spender, 1981; Weiler, 1988). As Sue Middleton points out, drawing on Freire, activist pedagogies are based on the assumption that people learn best by critically reflecting on and theorising their own actions in the social world. She documents the use of life-history analysis as a teaching technique in a women's studies course in an attempt to help students learn to link 'biography, history and social structure' (1987). Such an approach gives students the opportunity to interpret their own experiences in a way which reveals how these experiences have been shaped and influenced by the dominant culture.

Giroux (1981) argues that subjective awareness becomes the first step in transforming those experiences, and elsewhere he acknowledges that a radical pedagogy must take seriously the task of providing the conditions for changing subjectivity as well as changing broad political, economic and social structures. He writes: 'In short, an essential aspect of radical pedagogy centres around the need for students to interrogate critically their inner histories and experiences' (1984: p. 319).

However, it is important that the focus on the personal is a critical focus, and there are dangers in humanistic approaches which end up divorcing the social relations of the classroom from a viable political perspective. It is important when working with other oppressed groups, for example with Aborigines, to develop and encourage a sense of cultural and collective identity. Similarly, the key to empowerment for young women seems to lie in the development of a sense of *social* or *collective identity* as girls or young women—rather than merely in the development of a sense of identity as an *individual* (Gilbert (1988a) uses the term 'gender esteem'). In this way, by an exploration of the personal experiences and life histories of women, girls and young women can develop a strong sense of identity of themselves as women. A crucial aspect of all this, as has been argued, is to illuminate the interaction of the social and the personal on the one hand, and of history and private experience on the other.

There seems to be a further element involved in empowerment. As well as a critical awareness of a collective sense of identity there are skills and knowledge to be utilised in action. David Nyberg (1981) suggests that, as well as knowledge about power, people need relevant sources of information, processes of inference and skills of controlling information with which to 'challenge fate.' He writes that: 'The sense of self which one develops depends on whether one can even imagine long-term goals and whether one can develop skills to do the possible' (Nyberg, 1981: p. 173). Both Nyberg and Giroux refer to the role of 'the imagination' in relation to a vision of a future restructured society. Thus Giroux highlights the importance of 'human agency and struggle while simultaneously revealing the gap between the society as it presently exists and society as it might be' (1983: p. 30).

However, we have already indicated the difficulty of trying to teach students about ideology at a purely intellectual level. Subjectivities are constructed, as we have argued, at an unconscious as well as a conscious level, and the role of pleasure and desire, and fantasy, must be considered in the development of a feminist pedagogy. In the final section of this chapter we address aspects of such a pedagogy by offering practical suggestions for working with girls and young women.

Refashioning the feminine

Some of these ideas have arisen from our own experiences in action research and various school based projects in which we have been involved. We do not claim to offer easy solutions. As we have suggested, the issues being addressed are complex, and the development of appropriate and effective classroom approaches is not a simple matter. However, the following suggestions, which build on the theory and research we have outlined, seem to offer possibilites for practice.

A cultural studies approach

A cultural studies perspective, as developed by the Cockpit Cultural Studies Department of the Inner London Education Authority in Britain (see Bezencenet and Corrigan, 1986; Dewdney and Lister, 1986; 1988), is useful in developing activities to encourage girls to reflect on their own experiences, and on the experiences of women in their own families, and ultimately on their own futures. The Cockpit Workshop has been involved with practical photographic projects with young people both in school in collaboration with teachers, and outside, for example, with unemployed young people. Similar approaches could be used in various areas of the school curriculum with modifications according to the needs of the particular group concerned.

Andrew Dewdney and Martin Lister claim that the cultural studies approach allows ways of basing general educational practice on young people's views and experience, and emphasise that: 'Without conscious and active engagement with the content of young people's resistance, teaching is bound to reproduce more than it transforms' (1986: p. 31). Photography is central, though not indispensable to this approach, as it is a particularly useful means of representing and reconstructing everyday experiences and, through these activities, reflecting on them. The value of family photographs to help girls explore women's experience within the family, has been well demonstrated by an interesting project documented by Adrian Chappell involving a young unemployed working-class woman (1984).

This kind of approach was attempted as part of action research on the 'gender-inclusive curriculum' (Taylor, 1989a), in an inner city girls school in Melbourne with a large proportion of girls from non-English speaking families. The work was undertaken in connection with one class of sixteen year 9 girls (age range fourteen to fifteen years), together with one teacher who took the class for both English and human studies. The teacher, who was herself from a migrant background, introduced the 'family photos' project by bringing in her own photographs and talking about her own life history. This generated considerable discussion about the girls' own families and the memories of some migrant girls' countries of birth. The students were given the choice of working with family photographs or interviewing their mothers or grandmothers about their lives. The interview questions were developed by the girls, with a little help from the teacher and researcher, under the headings: Family and Home Life, School, Work, Spare time, Marriage and Children. The girls were also given the choice of doing photographic work themselves as in the Chappell (1984) project.

Initially the students were very interested in the project. However, although there were some successful outcomes, most girls chose to do rather unreflective work. They adopted a chronological approach in the production of their photographic panels, which was a preliminary stage in the Chappell project, and they were not interested in further extension into more reflective photo-montage production. It was disappointing that none chose to do their own photographic work, though equipment was available. One girl did achieve an interesting photo-montage of herself and her family relationships which was critically reflective. Another planned to do a photographic comparison of herself with her mother as a teenager, though she did not carry this through. Reflective work would perhaps be easier with older students, though year 9/10 is a particularly critical time in terms of educational and life choices.

The family interviews were more successful in terms of the aims of the project. For example, one Turkish girl interviewed her mother and clearly found it very worthwhile. She found that her mother had run away to escape an arranged marriage in Turkey and ended up having a discussion with her mother about sexism! The student searched for information about the region from which she and her family had come, talked about this to the class, and showed them a photograph and a map of the area. She also brought copies of her mother's year 4 report and passport, and an old document in Arabic script which had come from her grandfather. The written account the student produced was called 'Ganakkale and my Mum's Childhood', and this, along with the research involved, had clearly been very important to the student in relation to her cultural identity as well as to her gender identity. A similar approach has been used with some success in women's studies courses at secondary level (Dunn, 1985) and also in a women's history unit (see Ms Muffet, 1986: p. 30), both of which apparently generated considerable discussion between students and their mothers. Students could also become involved in oral history projects which focus on women's lives in their community. It would probably be most useful for this kind of work to be organised on a group basis.

One problem which arose in the action research discussed above was that many students did not regard their experiences and those of their families as 'legitimate' school knowledge. Some students did not consider the work to be 'real work' and did not really understand its purpose. It seems to be important that the approach is clearly framed, and that students themselves are involved in negotiating what is to be done. Student work needs to be carefully structured and monitored and the teacher has an important responsibility to direct students towards critical reflection through dialogue and questions (Freire and Shor, 1987). From the experience with the 'family photos' project discussed earlier, it seems that it is not enough to interact with the students and to monitor their work. Critical reflection needs to be encouraged through questioning, and this requires considerable time.

Popular cultural texts like the soap opera can also be a focal point for critical reflection. The initial phase of such work might involve helping students to reach an understanding of the characteristics of the genre and of a successful soap opera, including aspects of production and marketing. Given the polysemic nature of soap operas, which we discussed in chapter 3, teachers also have a particularly important role in highlighting the resistant or oppositional readings which can be made of soap operas when analytical work is being undertaken.

For instance, in implementing a unit on soap operas in a mixed year 10 English class at Hillview school (see chapter 3), the prime-time soap opera *Home and Away* was chosen for study and then compared with the daytime soap *Days of Our Lives*. The students then followed this by group work which involved developing new soap opera texts using their understandings of the genre. In this way they were able to become involved in the construction of alternative texts which better articulated their interests and experiences. Depending on the available time, girls could actually make a videotape of an episode of their soap opera, write scripts, or construct promotional material about the new soap opera. This last approach would involve research of marketing and promotional aspects of popular cultural texts, as well as consideration of the conventions of the setting, plots, characters and casting. It seems desirable that students go beyond critical analysis and become involved in this kind of cultural production, which allows students to explore the issues through fantasy as well as through more conventional approaches. As we have argued elsewhere in this book, the process of making an alternative text becomes a richer refashioning activity if students have acquired some understanding of the roots of the generic conventions they work with, and an understanding of the way in which such roots are ideologically constructed.

A rather different approach to the use of popular cultural texts has been suggested by Janice Winship. According to

Winship, magazines which have been produced in Britain to cater for the new 'streetwise' young woman of the 1980s are 'gender bending' in some interesting ways (1985). These magazines focus on men and boys as much as on women and girls, thus taking on questions of gender via masculinity. This could perhaps be a useful approach in the classroom where, for reasons we have discussed previously, questioning femininity is often perceived initially as threatening to teenage girls. Alternative practical approaches to the teaching of cultural studies are also documented by Anne Beezer and others (1986) who advocate that students develop theoretical understandings of popular cultural texts through research projects organised around topics such as the control and construction of women's magazines, advertisements, and teenage fiction.

In relation to empowerment, it is important to go beyond the development of critical consciousness: 'awareness' is not enough. If collective consciousness is to be extended and developed into collective action for change, certain skills and knowledge are needed to make this possible. Therefore these elements must be considered carefully if a gender-inclusive curriculum is to be effective. It is also necessary to think about widening the range of discourses available to girls and young women, thereby extending the repertoire on which they draw in the construction of femininity. In particular, this means carefully considering the cultural texts which are used in the classroom, which are so often 'a discourse not intended for her' (Rich 1980: p. 243), and instead offering access to discourses *intended* for her. This is also a necessary base for critical reflection.

Discourses intended for her

In this book we have consistently argued that young women need to have access to discourses that may position them differently in terms of adolescent femininity, but we have also argued that this alternative positioning will not be an easy task for educators. Alternative positions not only run counter to much of what popular cultural texts rely upon, but they also run counter to much of the general cultural and pedagogical ethos of the school. In general terms, popular cultural texts and school classroom practices reinforce young women's experiences of growing up female.

Popular cultural texts, by their very commercial and mass nature, often serve to perpetuate dominant ideologies, and as we have argued in Part II of this book, the space available for resistance and reconstitution of these popular cultural texts is slight. The argument we have put in earlier chapters is that this space needs always to be explored and extended, and that alternative textual practices might go some way towards this exploration and extension. A little of what alternative textual practices might look like was described in chapters 2 and 5. In general terms, we have argued that we need to make alternative discourses available to young women, and that we can facilitate this through the textual *materials* that schools work with, and through the textual *practices* schools adopt to work with such materials.

In chapters 3 and 4 we demonstrated how attractive (and seductive) are popular cultural texts like soap operas and romance fiction for young women. The way in which these texts connect with the lived experiences of growing up as a woman in contemporary society gives them a particular potency and appeal, and it would seem that schools' efforts to have students 'see through' the ideology of such texts have been fraught with danger. Earlier in this chapter we described Judith Williamson's concerns about 'hacking at the...roots of...formed subjects'. Her discussion of a mixed-sex group working on magazine stereotyping (1981/2) indicated how easy it was for the lesson to deride and devalue women's worth. On a different, but connected note, it is interesting to observe how frequently reports of ideological textual deconstruction in classrooms are likely to be reports of romance deconstruction (Parker, 1985; Thomson, 1985; Christian-Smith. 1988). It would seem as if deconstructing the romance formula is not only a familiar, and therefore 'easy' task, but that the almost inevitable denigration of women which can result from such work in a mixed-sex classroom is also familiar and 'easy'.

As we reported in chapter 4, the introduction of contemporary romance novels into the classroom as set textual matter may not be appreciated by many young women. For committed romance readers, it might well represent school colonisation—and subsequent devaluation—of a particular and treasured aspect of girls' culture. For non-committed romance readers, it might well represent further pedagogical reinforcement of the need for 'academic' girls to separate themselves from female subcultures and learn to read, write and talk like men. The same could be said about the study of television texts in the classroom. Valerie Walkerdine (1986), for instance, argues that the analysis of popular television programmes in media studies courses in schools can present great difficulty for many students: 'What concerns me is how these...children ...are being asked to deal with their previous enjoyment of such things—a pleasure shared with family, friends and their general social and cultural environment. It seems that they are being left little room for any response other than feeling stupid, or despising those who are still enjoying these 'perverse' pleasures' (Walkerdine, 1986: p. 196).

Contemporary approaches to reading and language study in the classroom have, as we argued in chapter 2, made the introduction of popular cultural texts into classrooms a much more likely event than in the past. The very popularity of such texts appears to guarantee their relevance to children—as well as their potential for enjoyment—and the current emphasis on personal engagement with reading, and on the value of read-ing for its own sake, have obscured, to some extent, what it is that the books are about. Texts children like to read become the focus of language units in schools, and, as we saw in chapter 2, the content of such texts moves almost naturally to become the content of the language classroom.

This does, of course, pose some problems for classroom use of romance texts, and it is interesting to note the resistance of teachers to the use of such texts (Christian-Smith, 1988). The content of these books is so blatantly ideological—so blatantly stereotypical in its versions of femininity—that many teachers are reluctant to include such books on their class lists (Altus, 1984a). And yet the same concern is not voiced about a num-ber of other popular texts. Formula detection, science fiction and adventure are not addressed in this way—and nor are other specifically 'young adult' series like texts by Judy Blume, Nat Hentoff, Paul Zindel, S.E. Hinton, Robert Cormier. And junior fiction formula writers like Roald Dahl, for example, often receive accolades. The generic conventions that texts like this rely upon for their ready recognition and mass popularity are almost as easily deconstructed as are romance conventions, and yet they are not seen to be ideologically of concern.

The point that we have raised several times in this book is that the devaluing of romance fiction is a variant of the more general devaluing of women's experiences and women's texts across the curriculum. Romance fiction is devalued as a literary genre, because it is formulaic, ritualistic and closed. Romance fiction is also devalued as a subject area because it focusses on a set of supposedly women's preoccupations—love, emotions, the family, relationships, and the romantic inscription of the body. While the masculine inscription of the body becomes a serious story to respect and admire, the feminine inscription of the body becomes a silly story to laugh at and deride. On a more general scale, while male stories of war, of death, of individual alienation and the search for identity become the stories of universal value, female stories of love, of birth, of families and nurturing become marginalised 'women's' stories.

This inequality in the treatment of popular cultural texts would be significantly reduced if all texts were studied differently. If texts were dealt with in terms of their construction and production, then the speaking positions and the spoken subject positions that particular texts rely upon could be more readily associated with discursive power networks. Texts could then be placed in terms of how they function, particularly in terms of how they contribute to the construction of certain subject positions. Reading positions which will produce texts as closed texts can be read as sets of conventions— not as personal responses to literary experiences. As a result, the selection of some texts rather than others for school study or private reading can become the purpose of inquiry.

Why and how books are selected for school study has long been of interest to educators, but as we have argued in chapter 2, there seems little doubt that a consideration of the ideological content of material is not an issue that many teachers regard as significant (Gilbert (with Rowe) 1989a; Luke et al., 1990). In early literacy classrooms, in the junior school, and in secondary schools and colleges, book selections seldom acknowledge the need to have material written by and about women, or to have material which addresses women's lived experiences (Ryan, 1982; Gilbert, 1983; NATE, 1985; Lake, 1988). On the contrary, many of the book selections that are made present images of girls and women which are stereotypical and limiting (Mortimer and Bradley, 1979; Frith, 1981; Knodel, 1982; Kraus, 1985). The 'great tradition' which most girls will work with in schools will be essentially a male tradition, and as we saw in chapter 2, the reading practices that most girls will learn in schools will be male reading practices. Students learn to read the 'great tradition' as men have learnt to read the great tradition, and by so doing, they learn to devalue women's experiences and worth, and to regard male activity, male need, and male images of women as universal images.

We would suggest that there are two ways to work against

these traditions. One is to develop a critical approach to the naturalistic and personalist emphases in language study, and to engage instead in textual study which explores the construction and production of texts as social, cultural practice. Something of this approach has been outlined in chapters 2 and 5, and reiterated briefly above. The other is to make alternative texts and alternative reading positions available to young women, so that discourses that *are* intended for them do reach them.

Alternative texts are much more accessible now than they have been in the past. Nonsexist picture book lists are available (Bissland and Pittaway, 1986), as are guides for adolescent literature (Allard et al., 1984; Dellitt, 1984), and general guides for children's books (McGinnigle, 1985). A recent listing of such material for young children is included in Bronwyn Davies' study of pre-school children and gender, *Frogs and Snails and Feminist Tales* (1989: pp. 142–3). In addition, it is not unusual to find general overviews of children's and adolescent literature often include themes like 'heroines' (see Yates, 1986). Alternative texts are published at all levels of children's and adolescent reading, and the spate of alternative fairy tale collections now available provides interesting testimony to the possibilities of linking girls to discourses that were originally intended for them (Phelps, 1978; Williams, 1978; Lurie, 1980). By demonstrating the ways in which popular folk and fairy tales have been altered at various historical moments—so that gender relations of a period may be articulated—the work of Jack Zipes, (1983a, 1983b) and Jane Yolen (1977) has obvious potential for the classroom. *Changing Stories* (Mellor et al., 1984) realises this potential by offering a class workbook which assumes that stories change because they reflect—and reconstitute—lived gender relations.

The recent attention to the publication of Australian women's literature (see, for example, Hampton and Llewellyn, 1986; Spender, 1988; Adelaide, 1988; Gilbert, 1988b), has made a number of adult women's texts accessible to senior secondary school students, and several contemporary Australian women writers, who resist stereotypical limitations, have achieved considerable success in the children's and adolescent market. Notable among this group would be Mem Fox, Robin Klein, Nadia Wheatley and Gillian Rubinstein. *Possum Magic* (Fox, 1983), *Penny Pollard's Diary* (Klein, 1983), *The House that was Eureka* (Wheatley, 1985), and *Beyond the Labyrinth* (Rubinstein, 1988) are some of the better known of their titles.

In addition feminist publishing houses like Virago and The Women's Press have undertaken deliberate publishing ventures to provide alternative texts for young women. The Women's Press have produced the *Livewires* series, and Virago the *Upstarts* series. The introduction to Virago's new series claims:

> Virago Upstarts is a new series of books for girls and young women. Upstarts are about love and romance, family and friends, work and school—and about new preoccupations—because in the last two decades the lives and expectations of girls have changed a lot. With fiction of all kinds—humour, mystery, love stories, science fiction, detective, thrillers—and nonfiction, this new series will show the funny, difficult and exciting real lives and times of teenage girls in the 1980s. Lively, down-to-earth and entertaining, Virago's new list is an important new Upstart on the scene.

The Australian McPhee-Gribble's *In Between* series is a similar venture, in that it does try to work with contemporary teenage issues and to take on issues of gender, race and class.

While alternative texts like these are crucial in providing access to other discourses for young women—discourses which offer alternative reading positions and alternative subject positions—girls may need to learn alternative reading practices so that they can read these texts 'differently'. In her analysis of the way in which young girls are prepared for adolescent sexuality through pre-teen comics, Valerie Walkerdine (1984) warns of the difficulties associated with introducing young girls to alternative views and images through texts. She suggests that the 'simple realism' of much anti-sexist literature may fail, because it assumes a 'rationalist' reader who will change as a result of receiving the correct information 'about how things *really* are'. Instead she argues for the power of fantasy to understand the way in which some literature—notably preparatory romance literature—works more powerfully on the 'psychic organisation of desire'.

The psychoanalytic argument put by Walkerdine is that the constitution of femininity (and masculinity) is not fixed or appropriated, but 'struggled over in a complex relational dynamic' (Walkerdine, 1984: pp. 183–4). Cultural texts are obviously crucial in this struggle, and Walkerdine's concern is with the different ways in which such texts might operate: 'What we need to ask is how much texts operate at the level of fantasy. For some girls they might well provide the vehicle for an alternative vision, while for others they might, by stressing the one as alternative to the other, feed or fuel a resistance to the feminist alternative' (p. 183). Given this, it would seem important for a feminist pedagogy to be concerned both with the social construction of female desire—and with the way in which cultural texts differently position women in relation to such desire—and also with the role that cultural texts might play in constructing such desire differently.

This will necessitate not only alternative texts for young women—texts which move beyond simple realistic options of role models—but alternative textual strategies for the classroom, which move beyond simple realistic readings of the 'world' of the fiction. Texts can also be 'played' with, and practical approaches to such play can be found in *The Making of Literature* (Reid, 1984) and in *Writing with a Difference* (Reid et al., 1988). Writing and reading practices can then become the *focus* of classroom language work (Gilbert, 1989b). As we argued in chapter 5, language tasks which emphasise the personal may well disadvantage girls, for the discourses that prevail in the classroom, and that are accessible to the girls, may well not offer speaking positions of authority which will enable them to write as young women, of young women's concerns. The 'personal' that the mixed classroom privileges and often encourages is not a personal that women can identify with. Women's experiences and concerns, are, as we have argued, too often devalued. Learning to read and write against the grain—as we argued for in chapter 5—is therefore about learning to read and write against conventions that construct women in ways that are demeaning and restricting. It is, as we argued, about learning to read and write in ways that offer constructions of female subjectivity that are not fixed and static, but are dynamic and shifting. It is about learning to understand the discursive construction of subjectivity and the potential spaces for resistance and rewriting.

We have argued in this book that a refashioning of the feminine can play a crucial role in transforming patriarchal gender relations, and we would want to emphasise our earlier argument that, though strategies are needed to address broad structural inequalities, changes in the cultural sphere are of equal importance. In particular we have argued that a critical awareness of the social construction of femininity is an essential first stage for change in gender relations. Our aim in this work has been to explore the spaces that are available for such reconstruction in the classroom, and to suggest ways in which popular cultural texts might be read and rewritten so that the feminine may be fashioned in alternative ways. The argument we have made is that classroom possibilities do exist to offer girls alternative subject positions from which they might read and write differently; from which they might differently position themselves in relation to dominant patriarchal discourse; and from which they might fashion their own femininity.

Bibliography

Adelaide, D. (1988) *Australian Women Writers: A Bibliographic Guide* London: Pandora Press

Alford, K. (1984) *Production or Reproduction? An Economic History of Women in Australia, 1788–1850* Melbourne: Oxford University Press

Allard, A., Keane, C. and Lam, M. (1984) *What's a Good Book, Ms? An Annotated Bibliography of Non Sexist Adolescent Literature* Melbourne: Victorian Education Dept.

Allen, D. (1980) *English Teaching Since 1960: How Much Growth?* London: Heinemann Educational

Altus, M. (1984a) 'Sugar-coated pills', *Orana* 20, 2, 70–90

——(1984b) 'Sugar-coated pills: continued', *Orana* 20, 3, 119–37

Apple, M. (1982) *Education and Power* London: Routledge and Kegan Paul

Anderson, J. and Yip, L. (1987) 'Are sex roles represented fairly in children's books? A content analysis of old and new readers', *Unicorn* 13, 3, 155–61

Ang, I. (1985) *Watching Dallas. Soap Opera and the Melodramatic Imagination* London: Methuen

——(1987) 'Popular fiction and feminist cultural politics', *Theory, Culture and Society* 4, 651–58

Ashcroft, L. (1987) 'Defusing "empowering": the what and the why', *Language Arts* 64, 2, 142–56

Baker, C. (1986) *Yacker* Sydney: Pan Books

Baker, C.D. and Davies, B. (1989) 'A lesson on sex roles', *Gender and Education* 1, 1, 59–76

Baker, M. (1985) *What will Tomorrow Bring? A study of the aspirations of adolescent women* Ottawa: Canadian Advisory Council on the Status of Women

Bakhtin, M. (1981) *The Dialogic Imagination* Austin: University of Texas Press

152

Ballenden, C. (1984) 'Facing the Future: Careers and Girls'. Occasional paper no. 10. Melbourne: Victorian Institute of Secondary Education

——Davidson, M. and Newell, F. (1984) *Better Chances for Girls: A Handbook of Equal Opportunity Strategies for use in Schools* Melbourne: Victorian Institute of Secondary Education

Barnes, D., Britton, J., and Rosen, H. (1971) *Language, the Learner and the School* Harmondsworth: Penguin

Beechy, V. and Donald, J. (eds) (1985) *Subjectivity and Social Relations* Milton Keynes: Open University Press

Beezer, A., Grimshaw, J. and Barker, M. (1986) 'Methods for cultural studies students', in Punter, D. (ed.) *Introduction to Contemporary Cultural Studies* London: Longman, 95–118

Begos, J. (1987) 'The diaries of adolescent girls', *Women's Studies International Forum* 10, 1, 69–74

Berger, J. (1972) *Ways of Seeing* London: BBC/Penguin

Bezencenet, S. and Corrigan, P. (1986) *Photographic Practices: Towards a Different Image* London: Comedia

Bissland, J. and Pittaway, C. (1986) *Picture Books to Grow On* Melbourne: Prahran College of TAFE

Blackburn, J. (1982) 'Becoming Equally Human: Girls and the Secondary Curriculum', *VISE News*, 31, 16–22

Bottomly, G. (1979) *After the Odyssey: A Study of Greek Australians* Brisbane: University of Queensland Press

Bourdieu, P. (1977) *Outline of a Theory of Practice* London: Cambridge University Press

——and Passeron, J-C. (1977) *Reproduction in Education, Society and Culture* London: Sage

Bowles, S. and Gintis, H. (1976) *Schooling in Capitalist America* New York: Basic Books

Brown, M.E. (1987) 'The politics of soaps: pleasure and feminine empowerment', *Australian Journal of Cultural Studies* 4, 2, pp. 1–25.

Brunsdon, C. (1981) 'Crossroads: notes on soap opera', *Screen* 22, 4, 32–7

——(1986) 'Feminism and soap opera', in Davies, K., Dickey, J. and Stratford, T. (eds) *Out of Focus* London: Women's Press, 147–50

Bryson, L. (1984) 'The Australian patriarchal family', in Encel, S. and Bryson, L. (eds) *Australian Society* 4th Edition, Melbourne: Longman Cheshire, 113–69

Bullock Report (1974) *A Language for Life* London: Her Majesty's Stationery Office

Burgess, C., Burgess, T., Cartland, L., Chambers, R., Hedgeland, J., Levine, N., Mole, J., Newsome, B., Smith, H., Torbe, M. (1973) *Understanding Children Writing* Harmondsworth: Penguin

Burton, C. (1985) *Subordination: Feminism and Social Theory* Sydney: Allen and Unwin

Byrne, B. (1989) *Dolly Fiction Series: Editors's Guidelines*

Carlson, M. (1989) 'Guidelines for a gender-balanced curriculum in English, grades 7–12', *English Journal* 78, 6, Ocober, pp. 30–3

Carr, H. (ed.) (1989) *From My Guy to Sci-Fi: Genre and Women's Writing in the Postmodern World* London: Pandora

Caywood, C. and Overing, G. (eds) (1987) *Teaching Writing: Pedagogy, Gender, and Equity* Albany: State University of New York Press

Chappell, A. (1984) 'Family fortunes: A practical photography project', in McRobbie, A. and Nava, M. (eds) *Gender and Generation* Basingstoke: Macmillan 112–29

Children's Rights Workshop (1976) *Sexism in Children's Books: Facts, Figures and Guidelines* London: Writers and Readers Publishing Co-operative

Chodorow, N. (1978) *The Reproduction of Mothering: Psychoanalysis and the Sociology of Gender* Berkeley, California: University of California Press

Christian-Smith, L. (1987) 'Gender, popular culture, and curriculum: adolescent romance novels as gender text', *Curriculum Inquiry* 17, 4, 365–406

——(1988) 'Girls' romance novel reading and what to do about it', *The New Advocate*, 1, 3, 177–85

Christie, F. (1984) 'Young Children's Writing Development: The Relationship of Written Genres to Curriculum Genres'. Paper given at the Conference on Language in Education held at the Brisbane College of Advanced Education

——(1987) 'Genres as choice', in Reid, I. (ed.) *The Place of Genre in Learning: Current Debates* Centre for Studies in Literary Education: Deakin University, 22–34

Clarricoates, K. (1978) 'Dinosaurs in the classroom', *Women's Studies International Quarterly* 1, 4, 353–64

Connell, M., Davis, T., McIntosh, S., and Root, M. (1981) 'Romance and sexuality: Between the devil and the deep blue sea?' In McRobbie, A. and McCabe, T. (eds) *Feminism for Girls* London: Routlege and Kegan Paul, 155–77

Connell, R.W. (1986) 'Theorizing gender', in Grieve, N. and Burns, A. (eds) *Australian Women. New Feminist Perspectives* Melbourne: Oxford University Press, 342–57

——(1987) *Gender and Power* Sydney: Allen and Unwin

——Ashenden, D., Kessler, S., and Dowsett, G. (1982) *Making the Difference: Schools, Families and Social Division* Sydney: Allen and Unwin

Corcoran, B. and Evans, E. (eds) (1987) *Readers, Texts and Teachers* Milton Keynes: Open University Press

Coward, R. (1984) *Female Desire* London: Paladin Books

——(1985) 'Are women's novels feminist novels?', in Showalter, E. (ed.) *The New Feminist Criticism. Essays on women, literature and theory* London: Virago, 225–39

Cowie, C. and Lees, S. (1981) 'Slags or drags', *Feminist Review* 9, October, 17–31

Culley, M. and Portuges, C. (eds) (1985) *Gendered Subjects: The Dynamics of Feminist Teaching* London: Routledge and Kegan Paul

Davies, B. (1989) *Frogs and Snails and Feminist Tales: Preschool Children and Gender* Sydney: Allen and Unwin

de Castell, S., Luke, A. and Luke, C. (1989) *Language, Authority and Criticism: Readings on the School Textbook* Lewes: The Falmer Press

DEET (Department of Education Employment and Training) (1989) *Female Students* Higher Education Series, Report no. 1, Canberra: AGPS

Delamont, S. (1980) *Sex Roles and the School* London: Methuen

Dellitt, J. (1984) *Strong Females in Adolescent Fiction: An Annotated Bibliography* Adelaide: Sth. Australian Dept. of Education

Derrida, J. (1976) *Of Grammatology* (trans. G. Spivak), Baltimore: Johns Hopkins University Press

Dewdney, A. and Lister M. (1986) 'Photography, school and youth: the Cockpit Arts Project', in Bezencenet, S. and Corrigan, P. (eds) *Photographic Practices: Towards a Different Image* London: Comedia, 29–52

——(1988) *Youth Culture and Photography* London: Macmillan

Dixon, J. (1967) *Growth Through English* London: Oxford University Press

Dougherty, W. and Engel, R. (1987) 'An 80's look for sex equality in Caldecott winners and Honor books', *The Reading Teacher* 40, 4, 394–99

Dunn, A. (1985) 'Women's Studies', in STC: Social Education Booklet. Melbourne: Participation and Equity Program, 15–22

Dwyer, P, Wilson, B. and Woock, R. (1984) *Confronting School and Work* Sydney: Allen and Unwin

Eco, U. (1978) *The Role of the Reader: Explorations in the Semiotics of Texts* Bloomington, Indiana: Indiana University Press

Eisenstein, H. (1984) *Contemporary Feminist Thought* Sydney: Allen and Unwin

Eisenstein, Z. (1979) *Capitalist Patriarchy and the Case for Socialist Feminism* New York: Monthly Review Press

Evans, T. (1982) 'Being and becoming: teachers' perceptions of sex-roles and actions towards their male and female pupils', *British Journal of Sociology of Education* 3, 2, 127–43

——(1988) *A Gender Agenda* Sydney: Allen and Unwin

Fetterley, J. (1978) *The Resisting Reader: A Feminist Approach to American Fiction* Bloomington, Ind: Indiana University Press

Fichtelius, A., Johansson, I., and Nordin, K. (1980) 'Three investigations of sex-associated speech variation in day school', in Kramarae, C. (ed.) *The Voices and Words of Women and Men* London: Pergamon Press, 219–25

Fiske, J. (1987) *Television Culture* London: Methuen

——(1989) *Understanding Popular Culture* Sydney: Allen and Unwin

Flynn, E. (1988) 'Composing as a woman', *College Composition and Communication* 39, 4, 423–35

——and Schweickart, P. (eds) (1986) *Gender and Reading: Essays on Readers, Texts, and Contexts* London, Johns Hopkins University Press

Foster, V. (1984) *Changing choices: Girls, School and Work* Sydney: Hale and Iremonger

Fox, M. (1983) *Possum Magic* Adelaide: Omnibus

Freadman, A. (1987) 'Anyone for tennis?', in Reid, I. (ed.) *The Place of Genre in Learning: Current Debates* Centre for Studies in Literary Education: Deakin University, 91–124

Freebody, P. and Baker, C. (1987) 'The construction and operation of gender in children's first schoolbooks', in Pauwels, A. (ed.) *Women and Language in Australian and New Zealand Society* Sydney: Australian Professional Publications, 80–107

Freire, P. (1972) *The Pedagogy of the Oppressed* Ringwood: Penguin

——(1985) *The Politics of Education* London: Macmillan

——and Shor, I. (1987) *A Pedagogy For Liberation* London: Macmillan

French, J. and French, P. (1984) 'Gender imbalances in the primary classroom: an operational account', *Educational Research* 22, 127–36

Frith, G. (1981) 'Little women, good wives: is English good for girls?' in McRobbie, A. and McCabe, T. (eds) *Feminism for Girls: an Adventure Story* London: Routledge and Kegan Paul, 27–49

——(1985) '"The time of your life": the meaning of the school story', in Steedman, C., Urwin, C. and Walkerdine, V. (eds) *Language Gender and Children* London: Routledge and Kegan Paul, 113–36

Fuller, M. (1980) 'Black girls in a London comprehensive school', in Deem, R. (ed.) *Schooling for Women's Work* London: Routledge and Kegan Paul, 52–65

Game, A. and Pringle, R. (1979) 'Sexuality and the suburban dream', *Australian and New Zealand Journal of Sociology* 15, 2, 4–15

Gilbert, P. (1983) 'Down among the women: girls as readers and writers', *English in Australia* June, 26–7

——(1985) 'Stereotypes for the classroom: student teachers write sexist children's stories', *Australian Journal of Reading* 8, 1, 14–20

——(1987) 'Post reader-response: the deconstructive critique', in Corcoran, B. and Evans, E. (eds) *Readers, Texts and Teachers* Milton Keynes: Open University Press, 234–50

——(1988a) 'Personal growth or critical resistance? Self esteem in the English classroom', in Kenway, J. and Willis, S. (eds) *Hearts and Minds: Self Esteem and the Schooling of Girls* Canberra: Dept. of Education, Employment and Training, 167–83

——(1988b) *Coming Out From Under: Contemporary Australian Women Writers* London: Pandora Press

——(with Rowe, K.) (1989a) *Gender, Literacy and the Classroom* Melbourne: Australian Reading Association

——(1989b) *Writing, Schooling and Deconstruction: From Voice to Text in the Classroom* London: Routledge

——(1989c) 'Student text as pedagogical text', in de Castell, S., Luke, A., and Luke, C. (eds) *Language, Authority and Criticism: Readings on the School Textbook* Lewes: The Falmer Press, 195–202

Gilbert, R. (1989) 'Text analysis and ideology critique of curricular content', in de Castell, S., Luke, A., and Luke, C. (eds) *Language, Authority and Criticism: Readings on the School Textbook* Lewes: The Falmer Press, 61–73

Gilbert, S. and Gubar, S. (1979) *The Madwoman in the Attic: The Woman Writer and the Nineteenth Century Literary Imagination* New Haven: Yale University Press

Giroux, H. (1981) *Ideology, Culture and the Process of Schooling* London: Palmer Press

——(1983) *Critical Theory and Educational Practice* Victoria: Deakin University Press

——(1984) 'Ideology, agency and the process of schooling', in L. Barton and S. Walker (eds) *Social Crisis and Education Research* London: Croom Helm, 306–34

——(1986) 'Radical pedagogy and the politics of student voice', *Interchange* 17, 1, pp. 48–69

Graves, D. (1983) *Writing: Teachers and Children at Work* Exeter: Heinemann Educational

Green, B. (1987) 'Gender, genre and writing pedagogy', in Reid, I. (ed.) *The Place of Genre in Learning: Current Debates* Centre for Studies in Literary Education: Deakin University, 83–90

Griffin, C. (1984) *Typical Girls* London: Routledge and Kegan Paul

Grimshaw, P. (1986) 'Man's own country: women in colonial Australian history', in Grieve, N. and Burns, A. (eds) *Australian Women. New Feminist Perspectives* Melbourne: Oxford University Press, 182–209

Guiley, R. (1983) *Lovelines: The Fun, Quirks and Trivia of Romance* London: Zomba Books

Hall, S. (1981) 'Notes on deconstructing "the popular",' in

Samuel, R. (ed.) *People's History and Socialist Theory* London: Routledge and Kegan Paul, 227–40

——(1985) 'Signification, representation, ideology: Althusser and the post-structuralist debates', *Critical Studies in Mass Communications* 2, 2, 91–114

Hampton, S. and Llewellyn, K. (1986) *The Penguin Book of Australian Women Poets* Ringwood: Penguin

Hanrahan, B. (1984) *Kewpie Doll* London: Chatto and Windus

Henriques, J., Hollway, W., Urwin, C., Venn, C. and Walkerdine, V. (1984) *Changing the Subject* London: Methuen

Henry, M. and Taylor, S. (1989) 'On the agenda at last? Recent developments in educational policy relating to women and girls', in Taylor, S. and Henry, M. (eds) *Battlers and Blue Stockings: Women's Place in Australian Education* Canberra: Australian College of Education, 101–9

Hodge, R. and Tripp, D. (1986) *Children and Television* Cambridge: Polity Press

Hollway, W. (1984) 'Gender difference and the production of subjectivity', in Henriques, J. et al. (eds) *Changing the Subject* London: Methuen, 227–63

Hudson, B. (1984) 'Femininity and adolescence', in McRobbie, A. and Nava, M. (eds) *Gender and Generation* London: Macmillan, 31–53

Irigaray, L. (1985) *This Sex Which Is Not One* (trans. C. Porter), Ithaca: Cornell University Press

Jackson, D. (1980) 'First encounters: the importance of initial responses to literature', *Children's Literature in Education* 11, 4, 149–59

Jacobus, M. (ed.) (1979) *Women Writing and Writing About Women* London, Croom Helm

——(1986) *Reading Woman: Essays in Feminist Criticism* London: Methuen

Johnson, L. (1986) 'The study of popular culture: the need for a clear agenda', *Australian Journal of Cultural Studies* 4, 1, 1–13

Jones, A. (1988) 'Which girls are "learning to lose"?', in Middleton, S. (ed.) *Women and Education in Aotearoa* Wellington: Allen and Unwin/Port Nicholson Press, 143–52

Kaplan, S. (1985) 'Varieties of feminist criticism', in Greene, G. and Kahn, C. (eds) *Making a Difference: Feminist Literary Criticism* London: Methuen, 37–58

Kaplan, C. (1986) *Sea Changes. Essays on Culture and Feminism* London: Verso

Kelly, A. (1985) 'The construction of masculine science', *British Journal of Sociology of Education* 6, 2, 133–54

Klein, R. (1983) *Penny Pollard's Diary* Melbourne: Oxford University Press

Knodel, B. (1982) 'Still far from equal: young women in literature for adolescents'. Paper presented at the annual meeting of the National Council of Teachers of English Spring Conference, Minneapolis

Kraus, W. (1985) 'Cinderella in trouble: still dreaming and losing', *School Library Journal* Jan., 18–22

Kress, G. (1982) *Learning to Write* London: Routledge and Kegan Paul

——(1988) 'Barely the basics? New directions in writing', *Education Australia* 1, 12–15

Kyle, N. (1986) *Her Natural Destiny* Kensington: University of New South Wales Press

Lake, P. (1988) 'Sexual stereotyping and the English curriculum', *English Journal* 77, 6, 35–8

Lam, M. (1986) *Reading the Sweet Dream: Adolescent Girls and Romance Fiction* unpublished M. Ed. thesis, University of Melbourne

Langdon, M. (1961) *Let the Children Write* London: Longmans

Lather, P. (1984) 'Critical theory, curricular transformation and feminist mainstreaming', *Journal of Education* 166, 1, 49–62

Lees, S. (1986) *Losing Out. Sexuality and Adolescent Girls* London: Hutchinson

Lesko, N. (1988) 'The curriculum of the body', in Roman, L. and Christian-Smith, L. (eds) *Becoming Feminine: The Politics of Popular Culture* London: The Falmer Press, 123–42

Lingard, B. and Symes, C. (1985) 'The contribution of radical cultural practice to a socialist alternative', *Social Alternatives* 4, 4, 6–11

Livingstone, D. (ed.) (1987) *Critical Pedagogy and Cultural Power* London: Macmillan

Lovell, T. (1981) 'Ideology and *Coronation Street*', in Dyer, R. et al. *Coronation Street* London: British Film Institute, pp. 40–52

Luke, A. (1988) *Literacy, Textbooks and Ideology* Lewes: The Falmer Press

——and Baker, C.D. (eds) (1990) *Towards a Critical Sociology of Reading: Papers of the 12th World Congress of Reading* Amsterdam and Philadelphia: John Benjamins

Luke, A., Rowe, K., Gilbert, P., Gilbert, R., Ward, G. and Baldauf, R. (1990) *An Evaluation of the Implementation of Early Literacy Programs in Two Sites* Canberra: Curriculum Development Centre

Lurie, A. (1980) *Clever Gretchen and Other Forgotten Folktales* London: Heinemann

MacDonald, M. (1981) 'Schooling and the reproduction of class and gender relations', in Dale, R. et al. (eds) *Politics, Patriarchy and Practice* Lewes: Falmer/Open University Press, 159–77

Martin, J. (1985) *Factual Writing* Geelong: Deakin University Press
——and Rothery, J. (1984) 'Choice of genre in a suburban primary school.' Paper presented at Annual Conference of the Applied Linguistics Association of Australia, Alice Springs, NT

Matthews, J. (1984) *Good and Mad Women* Sydney: Allen and Unwin

Mayer, G. (1989) 'Painted dreams: serial form and Australian television', *Metro* 78, 10–14

McGinnigle, I. (ed.) (1985) *The Sugar and Snails Guide to Non-Sexist Books for Children* Fitzroy, Vic: Sugar and Snails Press

McRobbie, A. (1978) 'Working-class girls and the culture of femininity', in Women's Studies Group (ed.) *Women Take Issue* London: Hutchinson, 96–108
——(1980) 'Settling accounts with subcultures. A feminist critique', *Screen Education* 34, Spring, 37–49
——(1982) 'Jackie: an ideology of adolescent femininity', in Waites, B., Bennett, T., and Martin, G. (eds) *Popular Culture: Past and Present* London: Croom Helm and Open University Press, 263–83
——(1984) 'Dance and social fantasy', in McRobbie, A. and Nava, A. (eds) *Gender and Generation* London: Macmillan, 130–61

Medway, P. (1987) 'The student's world and the world of English', *Opinion* 16, 4, 10–19

Mellor, B. (1987) *Reading Stories* Scarborough, WA: Chalkface Press
——(1989) *Reading Hamlet* Scarborough, WA: Chalkface Press
——Hemming, J., and Leggett, J. (1984) *Changing Stories* London: ILEA English Centre; Scarborough, WA: Chalkface Press

Middleton, S. (1987) 'Feminist educators in a university setting: a case study in the politics of 'educational' knowledge', *Discourse* 8, 1, 25–47

Modleski, T. (1982) *Loving with a Vengeance: Mass Produced Fantasies for Women* London: Methuen

Moi, T. (1985) *Sexual/Textual Politics* London: Methuen

Moran, P. (1983) 'Female youth culture in an inner city school', in *Educational Research for National Development: Policy, Planning and Politics* AARE Conference Proceedings, Canberra, 281–90

Morley, D. (1986) *Family Television: Cultural Power and Domestic Leisure* London: Comedia

Mortimer, M. and Bradley, D. (1979) 'The image of women and girls in children's books', *The Australian Library Journal* April, 87–93

Moss, G. (1989) *Unpopular Fictions* London: Virago, The Education Series

Ms Muffet (1986) 'What my mother told me...*Ms Muffet* 29 October, 30–1

Murray, D. (1982) *Learning by Teaching*, Montclair NJ: Boynton/ Cook Publishers, Inc.

National Association for the Teaching of English (NATE) (1985) *Alice in Genderland* Sheffield: NATE

Neill, H. (1989) '"One of the mission blacks": growing up on a Queensland Aboriginal reserve', in Taylor, S. and Henry, M. (eds) *Battlers and Blue Stockings: Women's Place in Australian Education*, Canberra: Australian College of Education, 65–75

New South Wales Ministry of Education and Youth Affairs (1988) *National Data Base on the Education of Girls in Australian Schools* Sydney: Southwood Press

Norris, F. (1985) 'Classroom politics', in Raving Beauties (eds) *No Holds Barred* London: The Women's Press

Nyberg, D. (1981) *Power over Power* New York: Cornell University Press

Oakley, A. (1984) *Taking it Like a Woman* London: Fontana

OSW (Office of the Status of Women) (1984) *Meeting Young Women's Needs* Canberra: AGPS

Palmer, P. (1986a) *The Lively Audience: A Study of Children Around the TV Set* Sydney: Allen and Unwin

——(1986b) *Girls and Television* Sydney: Social Policy Unit, NSW Ministry of Education

Parker, J. (1985) 'Growing through literature', *Australian Journal of Reading* 8, 4, 236–45

Phelps, E. (ed.) (1978) *Tatterhood and Other Tales* New York: The Feminist Press

Porter, P.(1983) 'The state, the family and education: ideology, reproduction and resistance in western Australia 1900–1929', *Australian Journal of Education* 27, 2, 121–36

Poynton, C. (1985) *Language and Gender: Making the Difference* Deakin University: Deakin University Press

Pringle, R. (1983) 'Women and consumer capitalism', in Baldock, C.V. and Cass, B. (eds) *Women, Social Welfare and the State* Sydney: Allen and Unwin, 85–103

Radway, J. (1984) *Reading the Romance: Women, Patriarchy and Popular Literature* Chapel Hill: North Carolina University Press

Reeder, S. (1981) 'Sex-role stereotyping in Australian children's book of the year award winners 1950–80', *Reading Time* October, 10–16

Reid, I. (1984) *The Making of Literature* Melbourne: Australian Association for the Teaching of English

——(ed.) (1987) *The Place of Genre in Learning: Current Debates* Centre for Studies in Literary Education: Deakin University Press

——Cardell, K., Doecke, B., Howard, J., Meiers, M., Morgan, W., (1988) *Writing with a Difference* Melbourne: Nelson

Rich, A. (1980) *On Lies, Secrets, Silences* London: Virago

Roman, L. and Christian-Smith, L. (eds) (1988) *Becoming Feminine: The Politics of Popular Culture* London: The Falmer Press

Romatowski, J. and Trepanier-Street, M. (1987) 'Gender perceptions: an analysis of children's creative writing', *Contemporary Education* 59, 1, Fall, 17–19

Rosenblatt, L. (1976) *Literature as Exploration* London: Routledge and Kegan Paul

Rubinstein, G. (1988) *Beyond the Labyrinth* Melbourne: Hyland House

Ryan, D. (1985) 'Foreword', Johnson, T. and Louis, D. *Literacy through Literature* Sydney: Methuen

Ryan, V. (1982) 'Feminism and curriculum: a case study of ACT colleges and senior schools', *Ideas in Education* 1, 11–15

Samuel, L. (1983) 'The making of a school resister', in Browne, R.K. and Foster, L.E. (eds) *Sociology of Education* Melbourne: Macmillan, 367–75

Schools Commission (1975) *Girls, Schools and Society* Report by a study group to the Schools Commission, Canberra: AGPS

——(1984) *Girls and Tomorrow. The Challenge for Schools* Canberra: AGPS

——(1987) *The National Policy on the Education of Girls in Australian Schools* Canberra: AGPS

Sears, P. and Feldman, D. (1974) 'Teacher interactions with boys and girls', in Stacey, J. et al. *And Jill Came Tumbling After* New York: Dell, 147–58

Sheridan, E.M. (ed.) (1982) *Sex Stereotypes and Reading* Newark: International Reading Association

Shor, I. (1987) *Critical Teaching and Everyday Life* Chicago: University of Chicago Press

Showalter, E. (1977) *A Literature of Their Own: British Women Novelists from Bronte to Lessing* Princeton, NJ: Princeton University Press

Snitow, A. (1984) 'Mass market romance: pornography for women is different', in Snitow, A., Stansell, C., and Thompson, S. (eds) *Desire: The Politics of Sexuality* London: Virago, 258–75

Spender, D. (1980) *Man Made Language* London: Routledge and Kegan Paul

——(1981) 'The patriarchal paradigm and the response to feminism', in D. Spender (ed.) *Men's Studies Modified* London: Pergamon

——(1982) *Invisible Women: The Schooling Scandal* London: Writers and Readers Publishing Co-operative

——(1988) *Writing a New World: Two Centuries of Australian Women Writers* London: Pandora Press

——and Sarah, E. (eds) (1980) *Learning to Lose: Sexism and Education* London: Writers and Readers Publishing Co-operative

Stacey, J., Bereaud, S., and Daniels, J. (1974) *And Jill Came Tumbling After* New York: Dell

Stanworth, M. (1984) 'Girls on the margins: a study of gender divisions in the classroom', in Hargreaves, A. and Woods, P. (eds) *Classrooms and Staffrooms* Milton Keynes: Open University Press, 147–58

Steedman, C. (1982) *The Tidy House* London: Virago

Strintzos, M. (1984) 'To be Greek is to be "good" ', in Johnson, L. and Tyler, D. (eds) *Cultural Politics, Melbourne Working Papers 5*, Sociology Research Group in Cultural and Educational Studies, University of Melbourne, 1–36

Swann, J. and Graddol, D. (1988) 'Gender inequalities in classroom talk', *English in Education* 2, 1, 49–65

Taylor, S. (1986) 'Teenage girls and economic recession in Australia: some cultural and educational implications', *British Journal of Sociology of Education* 7, 4, pp. 379–95

——(1989a) 'Empowering girls and young women: the challenge of the gender-inclusive curriculum', *Journal of Curriculum Studies* 21, 5, pp. 441–56

——(1989b) 'Days of their lives?: popular culture, femininity and education', *Continuum* 2, 2, pp. 143–62

Thomas, C. (1980) 'Girls and counter school culture', in McCallum, D. and Ozolins, U. (eds) *Melbourne Working Papers* Sociology Research Group in Cultural and Educational Studies, University of Melbourne, 125–56

Thomson, J. (1985) 'Literature and life: the appeal of the sensational romantic novel', *Australian Journal of Reading* 8, 4, 229–35

Thorne, B., Kramarae, C. and Henley, N. (eds) (1983) *Language, Gender and Society* Rowley, Mass.: Newbury House

Thurston, C. (1987) *The Romance Revolution: Erotic Novels for Women and the Quest for a New Sexual Identity* Chicago: University of Illinois Press

Tuck, D., Bayliss, V. and Bell, M. (1985) 'Analysis of sex stereotyping in characters created by young authors', *Journal of Educational Research* 78, 4, 248–52

Tulloch, J. (1989) 'Soaps and ads: flow and segmentation', in Tulloch, J. and Turner, G. (eds), *Australian Television. Programs, Pleasures and Politics* Sydney: Allen and Unwin, pp. 120–38

Walkerdine, V. (1984) 'Some day my prince will come: young girls and the preparation for adolescent sexuality', in McRobbie, A. and Nava, A. (eds) *Gender and Generation* London: Macmillan, 162–84

——(1986) 'Video replay: families, films and fantasy', in Burgin,

V., Donald, J., Kaplan, C. (eds) *Formations of Fantasy* London: Methuen, 167–99

Walshe, R. (ed.) (1981) *Donald Graves in Australia* Rosebery, NSW: Primary English Teachers' Association of NSW

Weedon, C. (1987) *Feminist Practice and Poststructuralist Theory* Oxford: Basil Blackwell Ltd

Weiler, K. (1988) *Women Teaching for Change. Gender, Class and Power* Massachusetts: Bergin and Garvey

Wheatley, N. (1985) *The House that was Eureka* Sydney: Viking Kestrel

White, J. (1986) 'The writing on the wall: beginning or end of a girl's career?' *Women's Studies International Forum* 9, 5, 561–74

Whyte, J., Deem, R., Kant, L., Cruickshank, M. (eds) (1985) *Girl Friendly Schooling* London: Methuen

Williams, J. (1978) *The Practical Princess and Other Liberating Fairy Tales* London: Chatto and Windus

Williams, R. (1977) *Marxism and Literature* Oxford: Oxford University Press

Williamson, J. (1981/2) 'How does girl number twenty understand ideology?' *Screen Education* 40, Autumn–Winter, 80–87

——(1985) 'Is there anyone here from a classroom? And other questions of education', *Screen* 26, 1, 90–95

——(1989) 'AIDS and perceptions of the Grim Reaper', *Metro* 80, Spring, 2–6

Willinsky, J. (1987) 'Romanticism and the new literacy', *Curriculum Inquiry* 17, 3, 267–91

——and Hunniford, R.M. (1986) 'Reading the romance younger: the mirrors and fears of a preparatory literature', *Reading-Canada-Lecture* 4, 1, 16–31

Willis, P. (1977) *Learning to Labour* Farnborough: Saxon House

Wilson, B. and Wyn, J. (1987) *Shaping Futures: Youth Action for Livelihood* Sydney: Allen and Unwin

Winship, J. (1985) 'A girl needs to get street-wise. Magazines for the 1980s', *Feminist Review* 21, 26–46

Women's Bureau (1989) *Women at Work. Facts and Figures* July 1989, Canberra: DEET

Yates, J. (1986) *Teenager to Young Adult: Recent Paperback Fiction for 13 to 19 years* London: School Library Association

Yates, L. (1988) 'Does "all students" include girls? Some reflections on recent educational practice and theory', *Australian Educational Researcher* 15, 1, 41–57

Yolen, J. (1977) 'America's cinderella', *Children's Literature in Education* 8, 21–9

Zipes, J. (1983a) *The Trials and Tribulations of Little Red Riding Hood* London: Heinemann

——(1983b) *Fairy Tales and the Art of Subversion* London: Heinemann

Subject index

Author index

169